Quality Daily Physical Activities

MW00748258

Contents

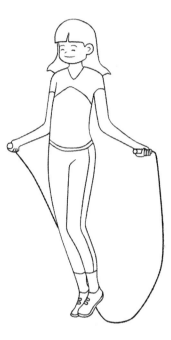

Physical Activity Summary Chart

Activity Name	Activity Level	Classroom	Multipurpose	Gymnasium	Outdoors
Sample Warm-ups or Cool-downs	moderate	X	X	X	X
Parachute Games	moderate			X	X
Obstacle Course Games	vigorous		X	X	X
Alphabet Pass	moderate		X	X	X
Red Light, Green Light	moderate		X	X	X
Stool Ball	moderate	X	X	X	
Don't Spill the Beans!	moderate		X	X	X
Newspaper Relay	moderate			X	X
Inside Out	moderate	X	X	X	X
Fine Feathered Friends Relay	moderate			X	X
Face to Face	moderate to vigorous		X	X	X
Concentrate!	moderate to vigorous	X	X	X	X
Opposites	moderate to vigorous	X	X	X	X
Beanbag Cross Challenge	moderate to vigorous			X	X
Teacher Says	moderate to vigorous	X	X	X	X
Fast Lanes	moderate to vigorous			X	X
Bump Tag	vigorous		X	X	X
Elbow Tag	vigorous		X	X	X
Chain Link Tag	vigorous		X	X	X
Reverse Tag	moderate to vigorous		X	X	X
T-rex Tag	vigorous		X	X	X
Amoeba Tag	vigorous		X	X	X
On the Lines Tag	vigorous		X	X	X
Blob Tag	vigorous		X	X	X
Enchanted Forest Tag	vigorous				X
Secret Tag	vigorous		X	X	X
Red and Blue Tag	vigorous		X	X	X
Tail Tally Tag	vigorous		X	X	X
Anti Tag	vigorous		X	X	X
Tunnel Tag	moderate to vigorous		X	X	X
British Bulldogs	moderate to vigorous		X	X	X
Boatmen, Boatmen	moderate to vigorous		X	X	X
Soccer-Baseball	vigorous			X	X
The Ladder	vigorous		X	X	X
Red Rover	vigorous		X	X	X
Crab Walk Soccer	vigorous			X	X
Hot Lava	vigorous			X	X
Crazy Card Challenge	vigorous		X	X	X

Physical Activity Summary Chart (cont'd)

Activity Name	Activity Level	Classroom	Multipurpose	Gymnasium	Outdoors
Balloon Games	vigorous	X	X	X	X
Ball Drills	vigorous		X	X	X
"Macarena" by Los Del Rio	vigorous	X	X	X	X
"Cha Cha Slide" by DJ Casper	vigorous	X	X	X	X
Electric Slide from "Electric Boogie" by Marcia Griffiths	vigorous	X	X	X	X
"Cupid Shuffle" by Cupid	vigorous	X	X	X	X
Cowboy Boogie	vigorous	X	X	X	X
Hoop Toss	moderate		X	X	X
Hoop It Everywhere!	vigorous		X	X	X
Through the Hoop	moderate to vigorous		X	X	X
Racing Crabs	vigorous		X	X	X
Beanbag Crab Race	vigorous		X	X	X
Single Jump-Rope Activities: Follow the Leader	vigorous		X	X	X
Chair Aerobics	moderate to vigorous	X			
Fitness Circuit Activities	vigorous	X	X	X	X
Yoga: Eagle Pose	moderate	X	X	X	X
Downward-Facing Dog Pose	moderate	X	X	X	X
Three-Legged Dog Pose	moderate	X	X	X	X
Mountain Pose	moderate	X	X	X	X
Crocodile Pose	moderate	X	X	X	X
Ragdoll Pose	moderate	X	X	X	X
Camel Pose	moderate	X	X	X	X
Shooting Stars Breathing Exercise	moderate	X	X	X	X
Frog Pose	moderate	X	X	X	X
Lion Pose	moderate	X	X	X	X
Fish Pose	moderate	X	X	X	X
Bow Pose	moderate	X	X	X	X
Dolphin Pose	moderate	X	X	X	X
Chair Pose	moderate	X	X	X	X
Flower Pose	moderate	X	X	X	X
Table Pose	moderate	X	X	X	X
Butterfly Pose	moderate	X	X	X	X
Plank Pose	moderate	X	X	X	X
Triangle Pose	moderate	X	X	X	X
Rainbow Pose	moderate	X	X	X	X

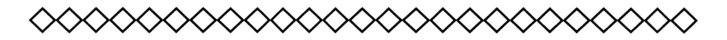

Quality Daily Physical Activities

Get students active as a regular part of the school day with a variety of easy-to-implement Quality Daily Physical Activities (QDPA) for different classroom situations. QDPA will not only contribute to the mental, physical, and social well-being of your students, but will reinforce the importance of being active as part of a healthy lifestyle.

Each QDPA break should include:

- a warm-up activity that includes stretching/and or a low intensity level
- a moderate or vigorous activity that increases breathing rate and heart rate
- a cool-down activity to help students gradually slow down and catch their breath

Use the QDPA Planner found in this book to help plan and get organized.

Warm-ups and Cool-downs

It is important to include warm-ups and cool-downs in all physical activity. Warm-ups help prevent injury to the muscles during physical activity, as cold muscles are more susceptible to cramps, tears, and sprains. Stretching and doing milder physical activities warms and stretches the muscles, making them more flexible and preparing them for more vigorous and sustained physical activities.

During physical activity, the muscles build up a fluid called lactic acid. Cooling down the muscles after physical activity helps to remove the lactic acid, resulting in less muscle soreness and stiffness the next day. Stretching after physical activity relaxes the muscles, improves flexibility, and returns the muscles, breathing rate, and heart rate to their resting state. Cool-downs can include the same activities as warm-ups, except they are done with lower intensity. Lower-intensity activities include stretches, as well as jogging or walking instead of running. Cool-down activities should be done for at least 5–10 minutes after physical activities.

Quality Daily Physical Activities (cont'd)

Ensure students participate in a range of daily physical activities that develop cardiovascular endurance, strength, and flexibility.

Endurance

Activities for cardiovascular endurance should be moderate to vigorous. These activities help the heart, lungs, and circulatory system stay healthy. They also provide increased energy.

Moderate activities: These activities cause an increase in breathing rate and heart rate. However, they do not cause enough of an increase that the participant cannot comfortably carry on a conversation during the activity. Examples of moderate activities include brisk walking, cycling, ball games, and dancing.

Vigorous activities: These aerobic activities increase the breathing rate and heart rate to facilitate cardiovascular conditioning. Vigorous activities can cause the participant to breathe heavier and more rapidly so they are unable to carry on a conversation during the activity. Examples of vigorous activities include running, aerobics, tag games, and fast dancing.

Strength

Activities for strength help build muscles, strengthen bones, and improve posture. To build strength, the muscles must work against some kind of pulling, pushing, or lifting resistance. It is a good idea to balance resistance activities that work the different muscle groups in the upper body, mid-section, and lower body. Examples of activities to improve strength include rope climbing, ball games, stair climbing, crunches, push-ups, and weight training.

Flexibility

Activities for flexibility help the body move easily, mobilize the joints, warm and relax the muscles, and reduce the risk of injury during more vigorous activities. Examples of activities to increase flexibility include warm-ups, yoga, stretches, dancing, gymnastics, and swimming.

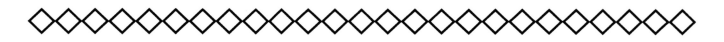

QDPA—Tips for Motivating Students

Strive to make QDPA breaks a fun and positive experience to motivate students. Students will respond more eagerly to activities when teachers are sincerely supportive, enthusiastic, and encouraging. Consider these tips:

- Develop the awareness of the importance of QDPA breaks by providing frequent opportunities for students to state and celebrate the benefits.

- Confirm that students feel comfortable about asking questions and discussing any concerns they might have.

- Create a safe physical and emotional environment so all students feel comfortable participating.

- Display a positive attitude and participate along with students, or model the required skills.

- Express genuine excitement for students' efforts throughout the QDPA break through gestures and motions. For example, clap your hands, or give a thumbs up sign of approval.

- Ensure that instructions are short and simple to maximize physical activity time and keep students engaged.

- Set realistic expectations for each student. Modify activities and skills as needed for individual students to maximize participation.

- Recognize and celebrate students when they do things correctly. Reward students with monthly teamwork and effort awards.

- Provide to students ongoing confidence-boosting, as well as specific skill feedback as they participate in a variety of activities.

- Choose activities and facilities that enable all students to participate.

- Afford students opportunities to learn concepts from other subjects kinesthetically.

- Challenge other classrooms to compete in sports activities.

- Implement ways for students to re-enter a game once they are "out." For example, allow them to move to a safe area, or complete an activity such as 5 push-ups and then re-enter the game.

QDPA—Inclusion of All Students

Ensure all students can participate in QDPA by modifying the rules of the activity, the equipment used, the use of space, or the complexity of the activity's skill. Begin by being aware of any pertinent information about physical limitations or other limitations a student may have. Here are some sample ideas you may use to facilitate the inclusion of all students.

Activity stations: Set up QDPA stations so a variety of activities are available to students at different skill levels.

Skill level: Plan for activities that do not involve a lot of specialized skill.

More chances: Give students opportunities for practice and allow numerous attempts to succeed in performing a skill.

Peer assistance: Assign a "buddy" to students, regardless of their abilities, to help build self-confidence and allow the opportunity for one-on-one teaching and coaching of the required skills.

Buddy-up: During running games, the buddy can run part of the way and the student can run the rest; in tag games, the buddy and the student can run separately but both must be tagged before they are out.

Modify spaces: Modify the size of the activity area and the proximity to other students to allow students with mobility difficulties to fully participate.

Slow down: Utilize larger, lighter, softer balls, such as beach balls instead of soccer or volleyballs, to slow an activity down and allow students more time to react.

Softer objects: Use smaller, softer, lighter balls to help students catch and hold the balls easier; use beanbags, foam balls, or soft rings for throwing.

Take breaks: Allow for frequent breaks in the activity.

Smooth surfaces: Activities should be done on smooth, hard, flat surfaces, such as floors or asphalt, to allow wheelchairs, crutches, or walkers to move easily.

Extend reach: Give a student a piece of foam or a pool noodle to extend their reach in tag-type activities.

Visual cues: Help hearing-impaired students by using flags along with the whistle to indicate when an activity is to start and stop, to let the student know when their name or number is being called, or to indicate that the music has stopped.

Brightness and sound: Help visually-impaired students by using equipment and boundary markers that have bright colours or strongly contrasting colours; have teammates identify themselves by using sounds, such as clapping, calling out, or wearing a wrist bell; for running activities, a guide runner can help the student by holding one end of a short rope while the student holds the other end of the rope as they run.

QDPA—Utilizing Different Facilities

Use this resource to plan QDPA breaks that are easy to implement, purposeful, and practical within a variety of types of spaces. Identify alternate spaces to use such as the outdoors, multipurpose rooms, hallways, or community facilities, and determine their availability in advance. When feasible, share appropriately large physical activity facilities with another class or group of classes. Work with other staff to coordinate schedules and plan as a team for QDPA. When using any type of space, ensure that students clearly understand the expectations for their behaviour and the consequences of disregarding the rules; you may wish to post the rules.

QDPA in the Classroom

- Organize the class seating plan so that it is easy to move desks, tables, and other objects to create an open space for free movement.

- Remind students to be aware of their personal space relative to other students and objects in the classroom.

- Ensure that floors are clean and clear of clutter before the physical activity starts.

- Establish a routine for ensuring that the classroom is safe for physical activity by designating specific spaces for QDPA.

- While students are still at their desks, provide them with instructions for the physical activity, then hand out any equipment required.

- Establish clear start and stop signals. Confirm that students clearly understand the meaning of each signal.

- Before QDPA begins, clearly establish with students rules regarding your expectations for participation in physical activity in the classroom.

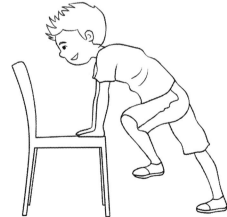

- Have students participate in on-the-spot QDPA and use music as a way to keep students focused.

- End QDPA breaks with a variation of Simon Says to calm students down.

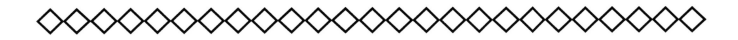

QDPA—Utilizing Different Facilities (cont'd)

QDPA in the Multipurpose Room

- Clear any obstacles from the room prior to using it.

- Establish a simple routine for entering and leaving the facility, for starting and stopping activities, and for handing out equipment. Ensure that students are familiar with the rules before leaving the classroom.

- Determine whether the equipment required for the activity is appropriate for the facility. If necessary, change to smaller, softer, or fewer pieces of equipment to avoid damage to the facility and injury to students, or modify activities so they can be done without equipment.

- Remind students that noise levels need to be kept low to avoid disturbing other classes.

- End QDPA with a calming activity.

QDPA in the Gymnasium

- Establish a simple routine for entering and leaving the gym, for starting and stopping activities, and for handing out equipment to be used.

- Divide students into groups before heading to the facility.

- Implement an emergency plan in case of accidents, and ensure that a first aid kit is nearby.

- Inspect students for appropriate physical activity clothing and footwear before leaving the classroom.

- End QDPA with a calming activity.

QDPA in Outdoor Spaces

- Establish a method for transporting equipment to and from the activity area; you can assign different students to be helpers, and use bins, net sacks, or cloth sacks.

- Provide instruction for the activity indoors to make sure you have students' full attention and that they can hear you clearly.

- When speaking, project your voice toward the back of the group.

- Arrange students so they are not facing the sun, or facing or paying attention to any distractions, so they can clearly see you and pay attention to demonstrations and instructions.

- End QDPA with a calming activity.

Involving and Informing Parents

Help parents gain a better understanding of how important physical activity is to their child's health and well-being. Here are some ideas that will help you accomplish this:

• Keep parents informed about the physical activities and games their child engages in at school, and involve them in their child's progress.

• Encourage parents to set an example for their child by actively participating in regular physical activity at home and in daily life.

• Invite experts to hold talks or workshops on physical activity and its importance to the growth of children, and invite parents and families to the event.

• Request that parents keep the school informed about the status of their child's health, and any physical activity their child participates in after school.

• Organize health-related physical activities, such as a sports day or family activity day, to promote cooperation and involvement between families, schools, and the community.

• Challenge families to limit the time their child spends on sedentary activities such as watching TV and playing video games.

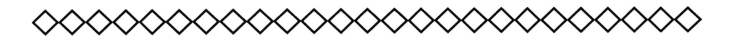

10-Day Physical Activity Home Challenge

Dear Parent/Guardian,

Quality Daily Physical Activity (QDPA) is essential for physical fitness and overall well-being. Research shows that students who are physically active on a daily basis perform better in school, have a more positive self-image, and learn good teamwork skills.

As part of our QDPA initiative, please take part in the 10-Day Physical Activity Home Challenge. Help to build your child's confidence, drive, and enthusiasm to make physical fitness a part of their daily routine for the rest of their lives.

Please record the physical activities your child and family took part in each day, along with the length of time spent doing the activity. Challenge your family to do at least 30 minutes of physical activity a day.

Here are some ideas:

- playing tag
- riding a bike
- swimming
- walking/jogging
- skipping rope
- playing sports
- aerobics
- dancing

Try some of the following activities and become more active as a family.

- Take a nature or city walk together.

- Visit the playground.

- Walk your dog, or a neighbour's or friend's dog.

- Start and nurture a family garden and grow everyone's favourites.

- Work together to complete household chores such as vacuuming or hanging and folding laundry.

- Visit the local swimming pool.

- Play with a soccer ball, football, or flying disk in a local park.

- Go on outings that involve walking, such as a trip to a zoo, farm, orchard, hiking trail, or museum.

- Join a community walk, fun run, or environmental cleanup activity.

Kindly return the Physical Activity Log to your child's teacher when completed. Your ongoing cooperation and participation is greatly appreciated! Your involvement is important!

Best regards,

_____

_____

Physical Activity Log

Congratulations on taking part in the 10-Day Physical Activity Home Challenge!

10-Day Physical Activity Home Challenge for the Week of _____

For the next 10 days, keep track of all the kinds of physical activity you do. Make sure to include such activities as walking, dancing, skipping rope, team sports, riding a bike, or playing outside. Can you do at least 30 minutes of physical activity a day?

Day	Physical Activity Description	Number of Minutes
1		
2		
3		
4		
5		
6		
7		
8		
9		
10		

How do you think you did? Explain your thinking. _____

_____

_____

Get Moving Brochure

A *brochure* is a booklet or pamphlet that contains descriptive information.
Create a brochure to promote the benefits of daily physical activities or exercise.

STEP 1: Plan Your Brochure

STEP	COMPLETION
1. Take a piece of paper and fold the paper the same way your brochure will be folded.	
2. • Before writing the brochure, plan the layout in pencil. • Write the heading for each section where you would like it to be in the brochure. • Leave room underneath each section to write information. • Also leave room for graphics or drawings.	

STEP 2: Complete a Draft

STEP	COMPLETION
1. Research information for each section of your brochure.	
2. Read your draft for meaning, then add, delete, or change words to improve your writing.	

STEP 3: Final Editing Checklist

☐ I checked the spelling.

☐ I checked the punctuation.

☐ I checked for clear sentences.

☐ My brochure is neat and organized.

☐ My brochure has drawings or graphics.

☐ My brochure is attractive.

QDPA—Sample Warm-ups or Cool-downs

Neck Stretch

1. Stand with your feet shoulder-width apart. Put your hands on your hips.
2. Without moving your body, and without turning your head, tip your head toward your right shoulder. Hold for 10 seconds.
3. Move your head back to an upright position.
4. Without moving your body, and without turning your head, tip your head toward your left shoulder. Hold for 10 seconds.
5. Move your head back to an upright position.

Side Stretch

1. Stand with your feet shoulder-width apart.
2. Raise your left arm over your head and let your right hand hang down at your side.
3. Slowly bend to the right, with your right arm reaching down the side of your leg, and your left arm reaching over your head toward your right side.
4. Bend as far as you can.
5. Hold for 10 seconds, without bouncing.
6. Stand up straight again, keeping your arm over your head.
7. Repeat with the right arm.

Upper Body Twist

1. Stand with your feet shoulder-width apart.
2. Put your hands on your hips and, without moving your lower body, twist your upper body to the left.
3. Turn your body back to the front.
4. Twist your upper body to the right.
5. Turn your body back to the front.

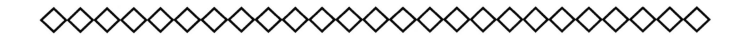

QDPA—Sample Warm-ups or Cool-downs (cont'd)

Shoulder Stretch

1. Reach your right arm straight out in front of you.
2. Bend your left arm and put your left wrist on the back of the upper part of your right arm.
3. Use your left arm to gently pull your right arm across your chest. Hold for 10 seconds.
4. Repeat the stretch with your left arm.

Upper Back Stretch

1. Put both hands behind your hips, palms facing out, and interlock your fingers.
2. Stand with your chest out and your chin down a bit.
3. Gently straighten your arms behind you, and slowly lift your arms until you feel a stretch.
4. Hold for 10 seconds. Relax.

Arm Flexes

1. Stand with your feet shoulder-width apart, and your arms hanging loosely at your sides.
2. Bend your elbows up and point them out to the side.
3. Raise your arms until they are level with your shoulders.
4. With your palms facing your chest, bring your hands together across the front of your chest until just your fingertips are touching. Hold for 10 seconds.
5. Open your arms out wide, still level with your shoulders. Hold for 10 seconds.
6. Bring your arms back down to your sides.

High Knees

1. Bend your arms at the elbows and hold your hands forward at waist height, palms down.
2. Run in place, bringing your knees up to touch the palms of your hands with each step.

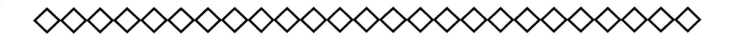

QDPA—Sample Warm-ups or Cool-downs (cont'd)

Walking Lunges

1. Stand up straight and take a big step forward with your left foot. Leave the right foot behind you.
2. Bend your knees slowly down toward the ground.
3. Keep your back, head, neck, hips, and right knee straight so they are all lined up.
4. Bend your right knee down so it is near the ground, but not touching.
5. Make sure your left leg stays straight, so your left knee does not go forward past your ankle.
6. Hold for 10 seconds.
7. Stand up and take a step forward with your right foot and repeat.

Side Lunge

1. Stand with your legs wide apart and your back straight.
2. Bend your left knee so the bottom of your left leg is in a straight line, with your knee directly above your ankle. Your knee should not be in front of or behind your ankle.
3. Keep your right leg stretched out, and keep your toes and heels flat on the floor.
4. Feel the stretch in the inner thigh of your right leg.
5. Hold for 10 seconds.
6. Straighten your legs. Repeat the lunge with your right leg.

Hip Stretches

1. Lie on your back on the floor with legs outstretched.
2. Bend your right knee up and leave the other leg outstretched.
3. Wrap your hands around the front of your right knee and interlock your fingers.
4. Keep lying flat on the floor while you pull your right knee toward your chest.
5. Hold for 20 seconds
6. Keep holding your knee while you move your knee back to the original position.
7. Stretch your right leg out fully again.
8. Repeat the stretch with your left leg.

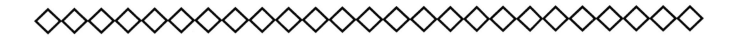

QDPA—Sample Warm-ups or Cool-downs (cont'd)

Straddle Stretch

1. Sit with your legs apart in a V shape.
2. Put one hand on top of the other with your arms outstretched.
3. Bend forward and stretch your arms and upper body over your right leg without bouncing. Hold for 10 seconds. Sit upright.
4. Bend forward and stretch your arms and upper body over the middle of the V without bouncing. Hold for 10 seconds. Sit upright.
5. Bend forward and stretch your arms and upper body over your left leg without bouncing. Hold for 10 seconds. Sit upright.

Standing Hamstring Stretch

1. Stand with your feet shoulder-width apart.
2. Bend forward from your hips with knees slightly bent.
3. Let your upper body, head, neck, and arms hang down loosely. Your arms should dangle near your feet.
4. Do not bounce or push yourself to touch your feet or the floor.
5. Stand up slowly.

Tricep Stretch

1. Raise your right arm above your head.
2. Bend your right elbow so your hand goes behind your head, and your fingers touch or reach toward the middle of your upper back.
3. Grab your right elbow with your left hand.
4. Gently pull your right elbow toward your left arm until you feel a stretch in the back of your right arm. Hold for 10 seconds.
5. Repeat with your left arm.

QDPA—Sample Warm-ups or Cool-downs (cont'd)

Calf Stretch

1. Put your forearms against a wall for support.
2. Stand with your right leg near the wall and your left leg extended out behind you.
3. Keep your heels on the ground.
4. Slowly bend your right knee down until you feel a stretch in your left calf muscle.
5. Hold that position for 10 seconds without bouncing.
6. Repeat with your left leg near the wall and your right leg stretched back.

Quad Stretch

1. Stand facing a wall and put your right hand flat on the wall to support your body.
2. Lift your left foot behind you, toward your bottom.
3. Reach back with your left hand and grab the top of your left foot.
4. Gently pull your left heel toward your bottom.
5. Loosen up your leg for a few seconds.
6. Repeat with your left hand on the wall and raise your right foot, grabbing the foot with your right hand.

Push-ups

1. Go on your hands and knees on the floor.
2. While still on your knees, walk your hands forward until your hips are stretched out. Your hands and arms should be aligned with your shoulders so your arms are straight below you.
3. Raise your body and knees off the floor so you are supporting your body only on your hands and toes.
4. Make sure your bottom is down a bit so your back, legs, and bottom are in a straight slanted line. Your bottom should not be above your back or down below your back.
5. Slowly bend your elbows outward to lower your body toward the ground, but do not touch the ground.
6. Slowly straighten your arms back up so you raise your body off the ground.

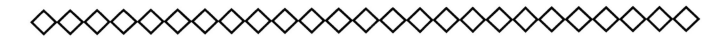

QDPA Ideas—Parachute Games
Activity Level: moderate

Parachute games are moderate physical activities that have an exciting and sometimes calming effect on participants. The billowing, graceful beauty of the parachute and the rustle of the fabric often induce feelings of amazement and awe. Parachute games encourage cooperation among participants and are a good base for noncompetitive play activities. Parachute games strengthen the muscles in the shoulders, upper arms, and hands, and help participants develop perceptual skills and rhythm. These high-interest games can be played indoors, but are particularly fun to play outdoors on a warm, sunny day.

Ocean Waves

Have all players grip the edges of the parachute on the ground, and shake it up and down with small movements. Pretend you are making ocean waves, sand dunes, a pizza with bubbling cheese, etc.

Popcorn Poppers

Have players practice lifting the parachute above their heads and back down in a fast, smooth motion. Then throw light balls on top of the parachute and launch them into the air

Toss It Off

Assign some players to grip the parachute edges and some players to stand around the outside. Throw a few balls or beanbags onto the parachute. Players holding the parachute must work together to toss the balls or beanbags off, and players around the outside work together to throw the balls or beanbags back on.

QDPA Ideas—Parachute Games (cont'd)
Activity Level: moderate

Jaws

Choose a player to be the first Jaws. The rest of the players will grip the edges of the parachute and hold it at waist height. Jaws goes under the parachute and holds one hand pointed upward above his or her head to look like a shark fin pushing against the parachute. Jaws moves around, while the other players make the sounds of waves and make waves with the parachute. Jaws moves quickly to "bite" a player by grabbing their leg and that player goes under the parachute to become a second Jaws. Now both players can grab other players. The game ends when everyone has been brought under the parachute.

Catch a Wave

Throw a beach ball on top of the parachute and have players move it around by making different sizes of waves.

Ball on Top

Divide players into two groups. One group goes under the parachute, while the other group holds the parachute at waist height. Toss a ball onto the top of the parachute. The players under the parachute use their hands, or lie on their backs and use their feet, to hit the ball off the parachute onto the floor. The players holding the parachute use their hands to hit the ball back into the centre of the parachute, but they cannot catch the ball and they cannot raise the parachute higher than their waist. When the ball hits the floor, teams switch places and the game continues.

Parachute Dome

Have players billow the parachute up and down three times. On the count of three, have them step under the parachute, pull it down behind them, and sit on it to seal the edges. The parachute will stay up for a few minutes.

Slippery Snakes

Place 3 to 5 short skipping ropes on top of the parachute. Direct all players to hold onto the edges of the parachute and billow it up and down. Instruct players to try to work together and to shake the parachute to get the "snakes" to fall off.

QDPA—Obstacle Course Games
Activity Level: vigorous

Obstacle courses can be an outstanding way for students to have fun while improving gross motor skills, balance, and coordination. Variety is key when designing an obstacle course. Try to incorporate opportunities for students to jump, hop, crawl under, climb over, crawl through, walk along, go right, or go left.

Obstacle Course

What you need:

Several objects players can:

- **go under,** such as chairs, tables, desks, benches, and a broomstick laid across two chairs
- **go through,** such as a pop-up tunnel and large open boxes
- **go around,** such as traffic cones and large balls
- **go over,** such as plastic hoops, and a "balance beam" made from a board lying on the ground
- **go across,** such as a "tightrope" made from a rope lying straight on the ground

Stations where students can complete a physical activity such as:

- 5 lunges • toe touches • 5 jumping jacks • skip rope • 5 crunches

Set up the objects. Here are two suggestions for games to play using an obstacle course:

Teamwork

1. Divide players into equal teams to compete against each other.
2. Have the next team member start when the previous team member is halfway through the obstacle course.
3. The first team to have all members finish the obstacle course wins.

Follow the Leader

1. Choose a player to be the leader.
2. As the leader makes their way through the course, they must call out a way to move, such as "crab walk," "swim through jelly," "flap your arms," "waddle like a duck," or "sway your trunk like an elephant." Everyone must move in that way.
3. After a few minutes, choose a different player to be the next leader and have the new leader call out a new action.

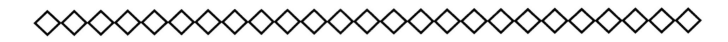

QDPA Ideas

Activity Level: moderate

Alphabet Pass

What you need:

- 1 beanbag

What you do:

1. Have players stand in a big circle with their backs to each other.

2. Give one player the beanbag. Tell players they will pass the beanbag to the person behind them, alternating over their heads, then under their legs.

3. Give players a chance to pass the beanbag around the entire circle once, then tell them they will now play a game.

4. For the game, players start from the letter A and name something that starts with that letter, such as an animal, a toy, a colour, an item of clothing, etc. Another possibility is saying a person's name that starts with that letter.

Note: It will be difficult to think of animals and objects that start with the letters Q, U, and X, so those letters may be skipped if necessary. Make a rule that players must take no more than 5 seconds to think of something that starts with the relevant letter. If they cannot think of anything, they must pass the beanbag on so the next player can try. If the next player cannot think of a name, the group can help.

Variations—Creative passing: Players can play the alphabet game while passing the beanbag to the person behind in any way they choose, such as over their head, under their arm or leg, at their side, with one or both hands, on their head, on their foot, on a fingertip, etc. Each person must pass the beanbag in a way that is different from how it was passed to them. Challenge players to see how many different ways they can think of to pass the beanbag.

Suggest a theme: Invite players to suggest a theme for the alphabet and stick to it as best they can.

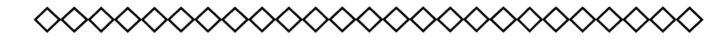

QDPA Ideas (cont'd)
Activity Level: moderate

Red Light, Green Light

What you do:

1. Choose a player to be the Stoplight and have them stand facing a wall or a designated line. Or, if the game is played in a field, have the player stand with their back to the other players.
2. The rest of the players line up side by side at a starting line about 10 metres away from the Stoplight.
3. The Stoplight calls "Green light" and the players try to advance silently and quickly toward the Stoplight.
4. The Stoplight can also call "Red light" at any time and everyone must freeze in place. The Stoplight turns quickly around and, if they catch a player moving, that player must go back to the starting line.
5. The first player to touch the wall or designated line without getting caught is the next Stoplight.

Stool Ball

What you need:

- 1 stool
- 1 volleyball or other medium-sized rubber ball

What you do:

1. Have players stand side by side to form a circle.
2. Place the stool in the centre of the circle. Choose one player to be the first Guard and have them sit on the stool.
3. Give the ball to a player in the circle. Have players pass the ball to the person next to them, around the circle.
4. Any player at any time may roll the ball at the stool to try to hit it. The Guard can use their hands, feet, or legs to make sure the ball does not hit the stool, but they must remain seated at all times.
5. To confuse the Guard, players can change the direction they pass the ball at any time.
6. If a player hits the stool with the ball, that player then takes over as Guard and the game resumes.

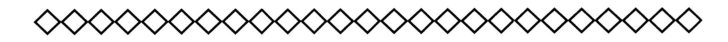

QDPA Ideas (cont'd)

Activity Level: moderate

Don't Spill the Beans!

What you need:

- 2–4 buckets or plastic bins
- 2 rulers
- 1 or 2 beanbags for each player

What you do:

1. Place two buckets with equal amounts of beanbags where you want the line to start. Place a ruler in each bucket.

2. About 7.5 metres away, place two empty buckets opposite the first two buckets.

3. Divide players into two groups and have them line up behind the two buckets containing the beanbags.

4. Players turn the ruler vertically, so it is pointing straight up like an Olympic torch, and place a beanbag on the end of the ruler. They have only one chance to place the beanbag on the ruler. Whatever way the beanbag ends up sitting on the ruler, that is the way the beanbag must stay until they drop it in the bucket.

5. Players run to the empty bucket, drop the beanbag in the bucket, then run back and hand the ruler to the next player. If anyone drops the beanbag on their way to the bucket, they have to start again.

6. The first team to move all the beanbags wins. The other team should continue until all beanbags have been transferred.

Variation—Running Water: This game is ideal to play in a grassy area outdoors on a hot day. Instead of beanbags, fill the two buckets with water. Players use a plastic cup to transfer the water to the empty bucket. It is okay if they drop some water on the way, but they must put at least some water into the bucket each time. If their cup is empty by the time they get to the bucket, they must start over. The first team to empty their bucket of water wins. Remind players to not spill water on purpose to empty their bucket faster.

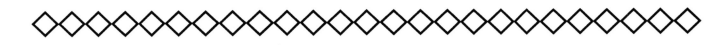

QDPA Ideas (cont'd)
Activity Level: moderate

Newspaper Relay

What you need:

- several old newspapers

What you do:

1. Establish a starting line and set up a finish line about 20 metres away.
2. Have players line up in groups of 4 or more.
3. Give 2 full sheets of newspaper to the first player in each line. Tell players that during this relay race, they must move to the finish line as quickly as possible. The catch is that no part of their body is allowed to touch the ground. Players must use the sheets of newspaper as stepping stones to get to the finish line by using their hands to move the sheets of newspaper one at a time and stepping onto them as they are moved, or by dragging the newspaper along under their feet.
4. The rules are as follows:
    - If the newspaper rips, they can use it as long as their foot doesn't touch the ground.
    - If the newspaper wears out to the point where it is unusable, the player must return to the starting line to get more newspaper and start the race over.
    - If a sheet of newspaper is lost during the race, the player can return to the starting line to get a new sheet and start over, or they can rip the remaining sheet in two and continue, as long as their foot doesn't touch the ground.
5. Once players get to the finish line, they pick up the newspaper sheets and run back to their team so the next player can start the race. Each player gets 2 new full sheets of newspaper.
6. The team that finishes first wins.

Note: This game is especially fun and challenging on a windy day. You can ask players who are not currently in the race to chase runaway newspaper, if necessary.

Inside Out

What you do:

1. Have players form a large circle and join hands.
2. Now tell them that, without letting go of each other's hands, they have to find a way to turn the circle inside out so they are all facing outward.

Note: This game tests players' cooperation and puzzle-solving skills.

QDPA Ideas (cont'd)

Activity Level: moderate

Fine Feathered Friends Relay

What you need:

• feathers, at least 1 for each group; paper plates, 1 for each group

What you do:

1. Establish a starting line and set up a finish line about 10 metres away.
2. Have players line up in groups of 4 or more at the starting line.
3. Give the first player in each line a paper plate and a feather.
4. Tell players they must move as quickly as possible to the finish line and back, while balancing the feather on the plate. After placing the feather on the plate, they must not touch the feather with their hands. If the feather falls or blows off the plate, the player can attempt to catch the feather with the plate but must not use their hands. If the feather touches the ground, the player must pick it up and start the race over.
5. Once a player reaches the finish line, the next player can start.

Note: This game can be played indoors, but playing it outdoors on a calm day adds the fun and unpredictability of light breezes blowing the feather off the plate.

Face to Face

What you do:

1. Have players choose a partner.
2. Explain that players will stand with their partners in the positions you call out. When you call "Change," they will quickly change partners. When they have a new partner, players must take the same position they were in last.
3. Call out "face to face," and make sure partners face each other. Then call out "shoulder to shoulder," "back to back," "head to head," etc.
4. After every 5 directions, call out "Change" so players have to find a new partner. If necessary, remind players to get in the same position they were in last.
5. Matchups can include elbow to elbow, knee to knee, toe to toe, hip to hip, finger to finger, and so on.

Variation: Change the rules so the body parts no longer match. Say "elbow to hip," "finger to head," "shoulder to back," "foot to hand," and so on.

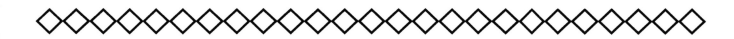

QDPA Ideas (cont'd)
Activity Level: moderate

Concentrate!

What you need:

- 10 volleyballs

What you do:

1. Divide players into groups of up to 10 and have each group form a circle.
2. Give the ball to one player in each group. That player must name a player in the group and throw the ball to that player. That player must catch the ball, then name another player in the group and throw the ball to them. Each player must always throw the ball to the same player, so each player receives the ball from the same player every time.
3. After players are used to the pattern of who they throw to, add a second ball and have them continue in the same manner. Once they are used to it, add a third ball. Then add a fourth ball.
4. When players are comfortable with the pattern, combine the circles to make one large circle. Start the game over with 1 ball and have players choose someone to throw the ball to, as before.
5. After they have gone around the circle a few times, add a second ball and continue as before. Then add a third ball, and so on.
6. See how many balls you can add to the circle and still keep things going.

Opposites

What you do:

1. Have players spread out around the room. Tell them this game involves doing the opposite of what they are told. Demonstrate the actions as players learn the rules.
2. Say "Up," and tell players they must sit or lie down.
3. Say "Down," and tell players they must stretch up as high as they can.
4. Say "Go," and tell players they must freeze in place.
5. Say "Stop," and tell players they must move by walking or running in place.
6. Practice the directions one or two more times, then start the game.
7. Call out any of the four directions and watch the fun!

Variation: This can be an elimination game.

Beanbag Cross Challenge

What you need:

- 3 beanbags for each team of 8 or more players

What you do:

1. Divide players into groups of 8 players. If you have an uneven number of players in your class, divide them into equal teams as closely as possible. The team with the extra player will be given a headstart.

2. Mark out the course by making Xs on the floor or ground. If you are outside on asphalt or concrete, you can use chalk. If you are inside on the floor, you can use masking tape. Mark Xs on the course for each team in a zigzag pattern as follows:

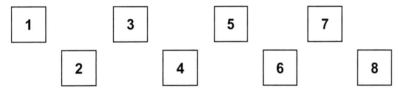

3. For each team, have the players stand on the Xs. Give 3 beanbags to Player 1.

4. At your signal, Player 1 throws the first beanbag to Player 2, who throws it to Player 3, and so on, in order down the line. Right after the first beanbag has been thrown by Player 2, Player 1 should throw the second beanbag, then the third beanbag, so all three beanbags are in play.

5. When Player 8 has all three beanbags, Player 8 runs outside the course to take over Player 1's position, and the rest of the players move one position farther down the course. So Player 1 moves to Player 2's position, Player 2 moves to Player 3's position, and so on.

6. Play continues until Player 1 is back in their original position.

7. This game can be a competition among teams for first place, second place, etc. Or you can decide to end the game when the first team has Player 1 back in position.

Teacher Says

What you do:

1. Have players spread out around the room. Tell players you will be playing Teacher Says, which is similar to Simon Says. Ask whether anyone does not know how to play Simon Says, and explain the game if necessary.

2. Model a variety of bends and stretches, such as twisting at the waist, bending over backward from the waist, touching toes, curling up in a ball, doing jumping jacks, or balancing on one foot. As players pick up on what to do, speed things up.

3. Every few instructions, do something totally different from what you say. Watch for players who do what you do, not what you say.

4. You can add yoga poses, and silly positions such as flexing your muscles in a muscle man pose or a scary monster pose.

Fast Lanes

What you need:

- several parallel lines on the floor, 2 per group of 5 or 6 players

What you do:

1. Have players line up in groups of 5 or 6 at the end of one line in each pair of lines. Make sure they know which two lines their group is using.

2. Tell players that, when you give the signal, they can move along the lines quickly in any way they want—running, hopping, skipping, galloping, flying like an airplane, and so on. They will move along the lines, tracing a rectangular shape and end up right near where they started.

3. Give players a chance to move along the lines for a few minutes, then ask them to stop moving.

4. Tell players that you are changing the rules.

   - When you call "Line," they are to change to the other line.
   - When you call "Action," they are to change the action they are doing.
   - When you call "Direction," they are to continue the action in the opposite direction.
   - When you call "High," they are to do the action while on their toes.
   - When you call "Low," they are to do the action while moving along as close to the ground as possible.

QDPA—Tag Games

Activity Level: vigorous

Tag games are good physical activities because they create a great deal of excitement and interest among the players. Tag games also increase the heart rate and breathing rate, develop gross motor skills and coordination, and exercise all the muscles of the body.

Bump Tag

What you do:

1. Choose one player to be "It" and one player to be the first Runner.
2. Have the rest of the players get into pairs and link arms with their partner.
3. Have pairs spread out so there is plenty of space between them.
4. The player who is It chases the Runner and tries to tag them. The Runner can go to any pair of partners, and link arms with one of the partners. The partner the Runner has not linked arms with is then bumped from the pair, and becomes the new Runner.
5. When the player who is It tags the Runner, they switch roles and the Runner becomes It.

Elbow Tag

What you do:

1. Choose one or two players to be "It." All other players find a partner, link arms, and scatter.
2. The two players who are It chase the pairs. To tag a pair, the players who are It must link arms with one of the players in a pair. When they do, the player they have not linked arms with must leave the pair and become the next It and chase other pairs.
3. Players who are It cannot tag the same pair they were just a part of.
4. The game continues until everyone is tired, or until you decide to stop it.

Variation: This variation is played like regular Tag, but players who have linked arms are safe. Players pair up and link arms, as above. The player who is It chooses 3 pairs to become unattached, and chases them. For those players to become safe, they must link arms with one player in a pair—they cannot pair up with an unattached player. When they link arms with a player in a pair, the player they have not linked arms with must leave the pair and find another pair to link with. If the player who is It tags a player, that player also becomes It and helps to catch unattached players.

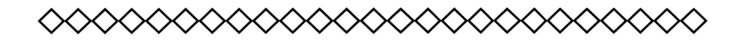

QDPA—Tag Games (cont'd)
Activity Level: vigorous

Chain Link Tag

What you do:

1. Choose a player to be It. Explain that when the player who is It tags a player, that player has to link arms with the player who is It. They are now both It, so they can both tag people. But they must keep their arms linked and move together.

2. Chains can break up into smaller chains at any time, but they cannot be fewer than three people.

3. Continue the game until only one person is not linked. The last person is the winner.

Reverse Tag

What you do:

1. Choose one player as "It."

2. The rest of the players count to 5 while It runs away.

3. The players then chase and try to tag It.

4. Whoever tags It becomes the next It and the game starts over.

T-rex Tag

What you do:

1. Choose one player to be the Tyrannosaurus rex. The rest of the players will be plant-eating dinosaurs or Herbivores.

2. Establish two safe zones about 20 metres apart. The T-rex stands in the centre between the safe zones.

3. Have the Herbivores stand in one of the safe zones. The T-rex lets out a roar and the Herbivores all try to run to the other safe zone without being tagged. If the T-rex approaches, a Herbivore can freeze in place. The T-rex can't see the Herbivore because he can only see movement. The T-rex must move to catch another Herbivore or roar to start the Herbivores running again.

4. The T-rex is not allowed to stand next to a frozen Herbivore to wait for them to move, But, if the Herbivore thinks they can run fast enough, they can make a break for it, even if the T-rex is standing right beside them.

5. If the T-rex catches a Herbivore, they switch roles and the game starts over.

Variation: If desired, you can allow the T-rex to stand next to a frozen Herbivore for the count of 5, waiting for them to move. If the Herbivore does not move during that time, the T-rex must move on.

QDPA—Tag Games (cont'd)
Activity Level: vigorous

Amoeba Tag

What you do:

1. Choose four players to be the Amoebas. Have two players link elbows to make each Amoeba, so the game starts with two Amoebas.
2. The partners in each Amoeba must work together to tag other players. When a player is tagged, that player links arms with the Amoeba that tagged them.
3. When the Amoeba has 4 players linked together, they must split into two groups of 2 players each so they make two Amoebas. Both Amoebas continue to chase other players, and grow and split as above.
4. The game continues until there are just 4 players left. Those 4 players can be the winners, or they can be the first Amoebas in the next game.

Variation: The Amoebas can start as groups of 3 players that split into two groups when they reach 6 players.

On the Lines Tag

What you need:

• gymnasium or tennis court that has lines

What you do:

1. Choose two players to be Catchers. All players, including Catchers, take any position on the lines and wait for the game to start.
2. Players and Catchers must all run along the lines, and must not step off the lines. If a Catcher tags anyone, or a player steps off a line, they move into the centre of the play area.
3. Other players are allowed to step off the lines and run to the centre to tap and free a player and both players then return to the game. The player who is It cannot tag players who are just about to step back onto a line.

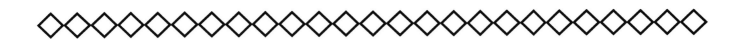

QDPA—Tag Games (cont'd)
Activity Level: vigorous

Blob Tag

What you do:

1. Choose one player to be the Blob.
2. Every player the Blob tags becomes part of the Blob. Players who are tagged must hold hands with the Blob and with each other to form a long chain. These players work together to catch other players, but only the players on the ends of the Blob can tag other players.
3. Players can run under the arms of the Blob to avoid being caught. The last player to be caught becomes the next Blob.

Enchanted Forest Tag

What you do:

1. Establish two lines about 20 metres apart.
2. Choose 2 players to be witches or warlocks. The rest of the players will be elves, fairies, or sprites.
3. Explain that the witches or warlocks must agree on a magic word that will make the players run. When the magic word is called, the players must try to make it to the other line without being tagged.
4. When a player is tagged, they must freeze in place and become an enchanted tree. The enchanted trees cannot move their feet, but they can move their arms and upper body to tag other players when they run past.
5. The last 2 players become the witches or warlocks for the next game.

Variation: Instead of witches, warlocks, elves, and fairies, players can be characters from a book or favourite show. Ask for suggestions and decide together who the characters in the centre will be and who the rest of the players will be.

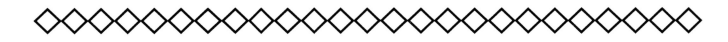

QDPA—Tag Games (cont'd)
Activity Level: vigorous

Secret Tag

What you do:

1. Choose 3 players and secretly tell each player what their role will be: Doctor, Chaser, or normal player. The Chaser must tag other players, and the Doctor can free tagged players.

2. Any player who is tagged must freeze until the Doctor unfreezes them.

3. Each round should last only a few minutes, until at least one player has been tagged and unfrozen.

4. After each round, 3 new players will be chosen and given their secret roles.

5. When each new game begins, the other players do not know which of the 3 players is the Chaser and which is the Doctor, and this results in some very lively gameplay.

Red and Blue Tag

What you need:

• flat item about 20 cm or 30 cm in diameter, red on one side and blue on the other (e.g., a frisbee, piece of cardboard, or paper plate that has paint or coloured tape on each side)

What you do:

1. Divide players into two equal teams. One will be the Red Team and the other will be the Blue Team.

2. Establish a centre line with two home base lines about 10 metres away from it on each side to be the team home bases.

3. Have the two teams line up on opposite sides, about 1 metre away from the centre line and facing the opposing team. Make sure they spread out so they have space to turn around when they have to run.

4. Flip the flat item in the air in the centre area, where players can see it. The colour facing up tells which team does the chasing, and the other team tries to reach their home base before they get tagged. Players who are tagged then join the opposing team.

5. Play continues until all players are on one team, or count to see which team has the most players.

Variation: You can increase the safety of the game by having players put cloth flags in their waistbands for the other team to grab, or tag each other with foam pool noodles.

QDPA—Tag Games (cont'd)
Activity Level: vigorous

Tail Tally Tag

What you do:

1. Establish two lines to serve as "pens" about 20 metres apart.

2. Give each player a piece of rope or cloth, and have them tuck it loosely into the back of their waistband as their "tail." Make sure players leave enough rope or cloth outside so it is easy to grab.

3. Divide players into two teams and select, or have players select, one player from each team to be the Catchers.

4. Have the teams line up in their respective pens. At your signal, players are released from their pens and Catchers try to snatch as many tails as possible. They may even accidentally snatch tails from their own team members at times, but that does not matter.

5. When a player loses their tail, they must return to their home pen and remain there. The Catcher from their own team can release players by giving them one of the tails they have snatched.

6. After a time, stop the game and have teams count all their tails, including the tails the Catcher is holding. The team with the most tails wins.

Anti Tag

What you do:

1. Choose one player to be "It." In this game, the player who is It can move around, but everyone else starts off stuck in place.

2. The player who is It goes around and tags people to unstick them. Unstuck players then hang onto It and try to stop them from tagging others. The more players who are unstuck, the harder it is for It to move.

3. When It can no longer move, It gives up and calls out the name of a new player to be the next It and the game starts over.

Note: Before starting the game, make sure players understand they need to be respectful of the player who is It. Tell players they are not allowed to pull It to the ground, and they should not pull or tug on It's clothing because they may cause damage. Players are allowed to grab It around the waist or by the arms. Monitor players to ensure they are not too rough.

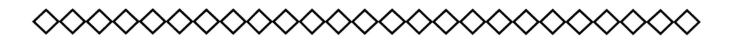

QDPA—Tag Games (cont'd)
Activity Level: vigorous

Tunnel Tag

What you do:

1. Choose 2 or 3 players to be Chasers.

2. Explain that when players are tagged, they must use their body to form a tunnel, then freeze. Another player must go through their tunnel to unfreeze them.

3. Have players demonstrate ideas for how they can form tunnels. If they are having trouble, suggest that they can get down on their hands and knees with their back arched, form a tunnel under their back in a crab-walk position, bend over at the waist so their feet and hands are touching the ground, or stand with their feet wide apart. Players going through tunnels cannot be tagged.

4. The game ends when you decide, or when all the players are frozen. The last 2 or 3 unfrozen players can be Chasers for the next game.

Variation—Double Tunnel Tag: Players hold hands or link arms with a partner and run together. Tagged players must form a tunnel together. Have players demonstrate ideas for how they could form a tunnel together. If they are having trouble, suggest that they can stand facing each other and join hands to form an arch over their heads or at their waists, get on their knees facing each other and join hands, or be side by side in any of the formations suggested in Tunnel Tag above.

QDPA Ideas

Activity Level: vigorous

British Bulldogs

What you do:

1. Establish two home base lines about 20 metres apart.
2. Choose two players to be Bulldogs and have them stand in the centre between the two Home Base lines. All other players stand together at one home base line.
3. The Bulldogs call out "*British Bulldogs, 1, 2, 3!*" and all the players run and try to get to the other home base line without being tagged. The Bulldogs try to catch as many players as they can.
4. Any player caught becomes another Bulldog and goes to the centre.
5. The last two players left become the first Bulldogs for the next game.

Boatmen, Boatmen

What you do:

1. Establish two home base lines about 20 metres apart.
2. Choose two players to be Boatmen. All other players stand together at one home base line.
3. The players call out "*Boatmen, boatmen, May we cross the river?*"
4. The Boatmen reply "*Only if you...*" then they say criteria, such as "*...are wearing red*" or "*...have brown hair*" or "*have blue eyes*" or anything else general or specific.
5. All the players that fit the criteria must try to run to the other home base without getting tagged. If they are tagged, they join the Boatmen in the centre and help to tag players.
6. The last two remaining players become the Boatmen for the next game.

Variation: The game is played the same, but catchers can be Crocodiles instead of Boatmen. So the players call out "*Crocodiles, crocodiles, May we cross the river?*" instead.

Soccer-Baseball

What you do:

1. Split players into two teams. Team 1 is in the field to start and players take the same positions as regular baseball.
2. Team 2 starts the game at bat. The rules are similar to baseball, except the players use a soccer ball that is rolled by the Pitcher and kicked by the Batter.
3. Outfielders run, throw, or kick the ball to the base before the Batter to try to get the Batter out.
4. Like regular baseball, there are 3 outs per inning and the game goes for 9 innings or until time runs out.

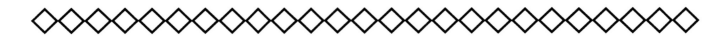

QDPA Ideas (cont'd)

Activity Level: vigorous

The Ladder

What you do:

1. Assign partners or have players choose a partner.

2. Have partners stand in two lines, facing each other. Have each player stand with their right arm outstretched to the side and move so they are standing arm's-length away from the player next to them in line. Then have players sit down facing their partner, legs outstretched. The bottoms of their feet should be touching the bottoms of their partner's feet. If you have an odd number of players, one can take the post of Caller.

3. Starting at one end of the line, have players count off.

4. The Caller says a number, and the partners whose number is called jump up and run outside the line of players to the end of the line. They get back to their place by running up the middle of the line as quickly as possible, stepping over the other players' legs as they go. When they return to their position, another number is called.

5. If you have an odd number of players, consider having the Caller take the place of another player partway through the game.

Red Rover

What you do:

1. Choose two players to become Captains for the two teams. Let the Captains take turns choosing a player each, until all the players are selected. Make sure there is a balance of size and strength on both teams.

2. Each team forms a line facing, and about 7 metres from, the opposing team. The players on each team hold hands to form a human chain.

3. The Captain who received the very last player gets to go first. The Captain says:

   Red Rover, Red Rover,

   Let [name of opposing team player] come over.

4. The chosen player has to rush the opposing team's line, and try to break through the players' arms. They cannot go under the players' arms. If they succeed in breaking through, they can rejoin their own team. If they do not break through, they must join the opposing team.

Crab Walk Soccer

What you need:

- 4 pylons or something similar to use for goal posts
- soccer ball, basketball, or beach ball

What you do:

1. Set up a goal area at each end of a designated area outdoors, or in the gymnasium.
2. Tell players they will play a game of soccer by crab walking to move and to kick the ball.
3. Divide players into two teams and start each at opposite sides of the playing field. Have one player from each team come into the centre for the first kick. Drop the ball for them to start the game. Referee the game and keep track of the goals.
4. The team with the most goals at the end of the game wins. Or you can set a maximum number of goals to achieve (e.g., 4 goals), at which time the game will end.

Hot Lava

What you need:

- 20–30 mats, preferably nonslip

What you do:

1. Arrange the mats on the floor so they are all facing in a variety of directions. The mats should cover most of the play area. The mats should be close enough that players can jump from one to the other, but not so close that they can simply step across.
2. Divide the players into 4 or 5 groups and start each group at a different location.
3. Tell players the mats are slabs of rock floating on a sea of hot lava. Once the players step onto the first mat, they will be in great danger. Players must travel by jumping from mat to mat, without stepping into the lava. If they step into the lava, they must start over.
4. Remind players to be careful not to accidentally knock their fellow travellers off the mats.

Variation: This game can be turned into a competition by arranging the mats in such a way that they still cross paths, but there are several starting points and ending points. The first team to get across the lava wins.

QDPA Ideas (cont'd)
Activity Level: vigorous

Crazy Card Challenge

What you need:
- 4–6 decks of playing cards

What you do:

1. Divide players into groups of 4 to 6. Place the decks of cards up off the floor in several locations around the room.

2. Have one player in each group draw one card from a nearby deck of cards. The suit of the card tells players where they go for the game and how they get there. For example,

   - **Diamonds**: crabwalk to the top-right corner of the play area
   - **Hearts:** skip to the centre of the play area
   - **Spades**: jog to the top-left corner
   - **Clubs**: hop to an object in the area (you choose which object)

3. Instruct students to perform a specific activity for each number on the cards. For example,

   - Ace – 1 star jump
   - 2 – 2 walking lunges (right leg forward, lunge, step so the left leg is forward, lunge)
   - 3 – 3 crunches
   - 4 – 4 criss-cross jumps (jump while crossing your feet, jump again and switch feet)
   - 5 – 5 tuck jumps (knees together high in front when jumping, quickly grab knees, let go)
   - 6 – 6 jumping jacks
   - 7 – 7 high-knees (jog on the spot with high knees for the count of 7)
   - 8 – 8 dribbles (bounce the ball 8 times)
   - 9 – 5 crunches
   - 10 – 10 toe touches
   - Jack – 5 walking lunges
   - King – 3 push-ups
   - Queen – 4 squats

Note: You may wish to put up few posters in view listing the cards and the activities that go with each card.

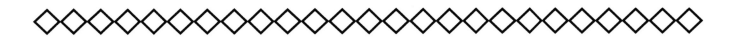

QDPA—Balloon Games
Activity Level: moderate to vigorous

What you need:

- inflated balloons, one for each player plus a few extra in case of breakage

What you do:

Keep It Up: Have players use their hands to keep the balloon up and off the floor. They must not hold the balloon, and they must keep it moving.

No Hands: Tell players they must find ways to keep the balloon off the floor without using their hands. If they have trouble thinking of ways to do this, ask for suggestions first. If necessary, suggest that they can use their breath, head, knees, feet, elbows, and arms.

Keep It Up Pairs: Have players choose a partner, or you can assign partners. Have partners stand toe to toe, then tell them to each take one step backward so they are moving away from each other. Tell them that will be their home spot. From that position, they bop the balloon back and forth to each other and try to keep it off the floor. They must always keep at least one foot on their home spot, but they are allowed to lean, and to use just one foot to take a step forward, backward, or sideways. After a few minutes, have them take another step backward. That becomes their new home spot. The fun is in seeing how far apart partners can be while still hitting the balloon. This could also be a elimination game in which teams that drop the balloon are out.

Balloon Challenge: Have players get into teams of 6, and have each team stand in a circle. Tell players they will each need their own balloons for this game. Have the players count off. When everyone has their number, call out a number between 1 and 6. That player will be the first to think of a challenge for another player to complete. Players should start with simple challenges, such as "Carrie, touch your toes." Carrie must then bop her balloon up in the air, touch her toes, and catch the balloon before it hits the floor. Carrie will then be the next person to give a challenge. After everyone has completed a challenge, tell players to make them a bit more difficult so they require more time. For example, they might say "Turn around and touch the ground." The player doing the challenge must bop the balloon higher to complete the challenge in time. Then have players make challenges even harder, such as "High five everyone." or "Do 10 jumping jacks."

QDPA—Ball Drills
Activity Level: moderate to vigorous

Basketball

Dribbling: With one hand, bounce the ball in place, then bounce the ball while walking, then while jogging. You may wish to create a path for students to follow.

Crossovers: Bounce the ball from one hand to the other hand and back. Try dribbling the ball from one hand to the other while walking forward.

Two Balls: Bounce two balls at the same time—one for each hand.

Two Balls—One High, One Low: Bend forward from the waist and bend your knees slightly. Bounce one ball low to the ground with one hand, and bounce a second ball in longer, shoulder-high bounces with the other hand.

Figure 8s: Stand with your legs wide apart and your knees slightly bent. Dribble the ball in a Figure 8 through your legs. Start with your right hand, and dribble the ball through your legs from front to back toward the left side. Take over bouncing the ball with your left hand. Bounce the ball around the outside of your left leg toward the front, then through your legs from front to back toward the right side. Take over bouncing the ball with your right hand around your right leg toward the front, and continue the Figure 8s.

Spider Drill: Stand with your legs wide apart and your knees slightly bent. Bounce the ball once with your right hand, then bounce it once with your left hand pushing the ball lightly through your legs toward your back. Without turning around, quickly move your right hand behind your back and bounce the ball once, then move your left hand behind your back and bounce the ball once, pushing the ball back through your legs toward the front. Move your right hand back to the front and continue. As you get used to the moves, do them faster.

Bounce Pass: Use two hands to bounce the ball to a partner with just one bounce.

Two-handed Chest Pass: Use two hands to hold the ball in front of your chest. With a quick thrust forward, push the ball toward your partner and let go.

   Chalkboard Publishing © 2013

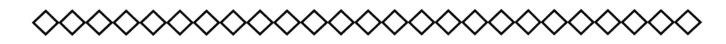

QDPA—Ball Drills (cont'd)
Activity Level: moderate to vigorous

Volleyball

Set-ups: Raise your arms and keep your elbows bent. Use the fingertips of both hands and quickly straighten your arms, using the force of your arms to push the ball up in the air. Try to keep the ball up for a long time. You can also try to make the ball go a little higher each time.

Volleys: Hold the ball with both hands and bend your elbows. Use your fingertips and quickly straighten your arms, using the force of your arms to push the ball toward your partner. Volley the ball back and forth with your partner and try to keep the ball up for a long time.

Serves: Hold the ball in the palm of your left hand and position the ball in front of your right arm at waist height. Bend your body forward a little and bend your knees. Hold your right arm down at your side with your hand open and your palm facing forward. Then swing your arm up high in back. Step forward with your left foot and bring your right arm forward quickly in one smooth swing. Hit the ball hard with your right wrist to knock the ball out of your hand and push it up in the air.

Soccer

Soccer-Slalom: Set up pylons and have students dribble a soccer ball around them in a zigzag pattern.

Partners: Assign partners or have students choose a partner. Partners kick the ball back and forth between them, and practice trapping the ball each time.

Goal Practice: Divide players into two lines in front of the goal. Have one line of players pass to the other line of players, who then kick the ball into the goal. After the line of players have all had a turn, have the lines of players switch places. Players can also take turns being the goalie.

> **Teacher Tip:** After practicing these drills, you may wish to divide students into teams and have a traditional game of basketball, volleyball, or soccer.

QDPA—Music and Movement
Activity Level: moderate to vigorous

Moving and grooving to music is an ideal way to get students active! Play a wide variety of musical styles. It doesn't have to be dance music, as long as students can move to it. You may wish to include such popular music as classical, 50s, 60s, 70s, 80s, disco, jive, hiphop, and country. To add some "spice," be sure to include cultural music such as African, Calypso, Spanish, Italian, Mexican, Irish, East Coast, Greek, etc.

Tips

- Ensure all equipment that is to be used during QDPA, such as CDs and a CD player, is in an easily accessible place so you can start at any time.
- Review with students a signal to begin or end an activity, such as a bell, hand clap, or special call-out phrase, and always wait for everyone to follow that signal.
- When choosing music such as pop music, be aware of the wording and meaning in songs. Preview such music and use discretion regarding appropriateness.
- Discuss with students the idea of keeping a "steady beat." Explain that keeping a beat means to be able to move or to tap a steady pulse, like the ticking of a clock or timer. This idea will help as students move with the music.
- You may also want to introduce and reinforce the following words:

  - *steady beat* – unit of measure of rhythmic time
  - *rhythm* – the combinations of long and short, even and uneven sounds that convey a sense of movement in time
  - *rest* – no sound during a unit of measure of rhythmic time
  - *tempo* – the pace at which music moves according to the speed of the underlying beat's movement in time

- Have students act or create their own movements to mimic everyday activities or objects to the beat of the music. For example

  - Brushing your teeth and getting ready for bed
  - Steps to making dinner
  - Picking up something off the ground
  - Moving like a robot
  - Acting out a sport
  - Pushing a grocery cart

  - Acting like a sprinkler or lawnmower
  - Acting like different animals
  - Vacuuming
  - Casting with a fishing pole
  - Swatting mosquitoes
  - Driving a car or other vehicle

QDPA—Fitness Dances

Activity Level: vigorous

"Macarena" by Los Del Rio

What you need:

- Song "Macarena" by Los Del Rio
- Music player

What you do:

1. Stand with your feet together, and your arms at your sides.

2. When the music starts, turn your right hand over so your palm is facing up and bring your right arm straight out in front of you. Keep it in place.

3. Do the same with your left arm. Keep it in place.

4. Bend your right elbow and fold your right arm across your chest. Place your right hand on your left shoulder. Keep it in place

5. Bend your left elbow and fold your left arm across your chest, over your right arm. Place your left hand on your right shoulder. Keep it in place.

6. Bring your right arm up and place your right hand on the back of your head. Keep it in place.

7. Bring your left arm up and place your left hand on the back of your head. Keep it in place.

8. Bring your right arm down and across your belly and place your right hand on your waist on your left side. Keep it in place.

9. Bring your left arm down and across your belly and right arm. Place your left hand on your waist on your right side. Keep it in place.

10. Place your right hand on your right hip. Keep it in place.

11. Place your left hand on your left hip. Keep it in place.

12. Make a circle with your hips 2 times.

13. Jump a quarter turn to the right.

14. Repeat the steps until the end of the song.

QDPA—Fitness Dances (cont'd)

Activity Level: vigorous

"Cha Cha Slide" by DJ Casper

What you need:

- Song "Cha Cha Slide" by DJ Casper
- Music player

Basic steps:

1. Move your body to the music until he says "Funky, funky, funky" a second time.

2. ["Clap, clap, clap your hands"] Clap your hands to the beat.

3. ["We're going to learn the basic steps"] Step to the right with your right foot, cross behind with your left foot, step to the right with your right foot, tap your left foot next to your right foot.

4. ["To the left"] Step to the left with your left foot, cross behind with your right foot, step to the left with your left foot, tap your right foot next to your left foot.

5. ["Take it back y'all"] Step back with your right foot, then back with your left foot, then back with your right foot.

6. ["One hop this time"] Hop once in place.

7. ["Right foot let's stomp"] Small step to the right, stomping your right foot down.

8. ["Left foot let's stomp"] Small step to the left, stomping your left foot down.

9. ["Cha cha real slow"] Step forward with your right foot, raise your left foot a little, rock back onto your left foot, then step your right foot back together with your left foot, tiny step in place with your left foot, tiny step in place with your right foot; step forward with your left foot, lift your right foot a little, rock back onto your right foot, then step your left foot back together with your right foot, tiny step in place with your right foot, tiny step in place with your left foot.

10. Repeat the steps as instructed in the song. The number of times you are to do the steps varies and the steps change in the song, so listen carefully!

continued next page

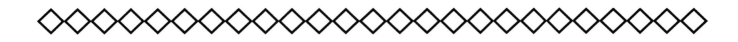

"Cha Cha Slide" by DJ Casper (cont'd)

Other steps:

Turn it out (optional): When taking the first step in the next sequence, turn your body a quarter turn to the left. (This part can be omitted so the dance is all done facing one direction.)

Charlie Brown: Step-bounce forward with your right foot, lift your left foot off the ground a little, step-bounce back onto your left foot, lift your right foot a little. Do this twice with a bounce in your step.

Slide to the left: Big step to the left with your left foot, then slide your right foot over beside it. Do the opposite for "Slide to the right."

Criss-cross: ["Criss"] Do a little jump, crossing your right foot in front of your left foot and crossing your left foot behind your right foot before you land. ["Cross"] Do another little jump, uncrossing your feet before you land.

Hands on your knees: Bend your knees, put your hands on your knees, move your knees together and apart, while crossing and uncrossing your arms and sliding your hands to the opposite knee and back again.

Get funky with it: Move any way you like.

Freeze: Freeze in the place.

How low can you go: Set your feet wide apart, sway your body side to side while you bend your knees down. Keep going down lower and lower as instructed.

Can you bring it to the top: Pretend you are climbing a ladder with your hands and slowly stand upright as you climb.

Reverse: Turn your body to hop in place once to the right, then hop-turn back to the front. Then turn your body to hop in place once to the left, then hop-turn back to the front.

Teacher Tip: Challenge students to create their own fitness dance and share with the class.

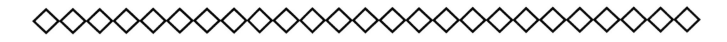

QDPA—Fitness Dances (cont'd)

Activity Level: vigorous

Electric Slide from "Electric Boogie" by Marcia Griffiths

What you need:

- Song "Electric Boogie" by Marcia Griffiths
- Music player

Basic steps:

1. Step to the right, step your left foot over beside your right foot. Repeat. With each step in this dance, move your arms, bend your knees, and bounce a little to groove to the beat.
2. Step to the left, step your right foot over beside your left foot. Repeat.
3. Turn your body to the right a bit and step back with your right foot. Bring your left foot back beside your right foot. Repeat.
4. Step forward with your left foot. Bring your right foot forward and tap your toes beside your left foot.
5. Step back with your right foot. Bring your left foot back and tap your toes beside your right foot.
6. Step forward with your left foot. Scoop your right foot along the ground. Lift your right foot up high while you swivel on your left foot to make a quarter turn to the left.
7. Put your right foot down, and repeat all the steps until the end of the song.

"Cupid Shuffle" by Cupid

What you need:

- Song "Cupid Shuffle" by Cupid
- Music player

Basic steps:

1. Boogie to the music while the singer says "Cupid Shuffle" over and over again. Start the dance on "Down, down, do your dance, do your dance."
2. Step to the right on your right foot, step your left foot beside your right foot. Repeat 3 more times.
3. Step to the left on your left foot, step your right foot beside your left foot. Repeat 3 more times.
4. Tap your right heel forward, put your right foot back beside your left foot. Tap your left heel forward, put your left foot back beside your right. Repeat.
5. Twist your hips and feet to the right 4 steps while turning your body a quarter turn to the right.
6. Repeat the steps until the song ends. Clap your hands and move your arms and hips as you dance. Put a bounce in your steps!

Cowboy Boogie

- Suggested music: various country music songs, for example, "Up" by Shania Twain
- Music player

Basic steps:

1. Take one step to the right with your right foot, cross your left foot behind your right foot, step to the right with your right foot, "hitch" (lift) your left knee up.

2. Take one step to the left with your left foot, cross your right foot behind your left foot, step to the left with your left foot, hitch your right knee up.

3. Step forward with your left foot, hitch your right knee up, step forward with your right foot, hitch your left knee up.

4. Step back with your right foot, step back with your left foot, step back with your right foot, then hitch your left knee up.

5. Step your left foot forward and leave it in place. Turn your body to the right a little. Bend your knees slightly and boogie (bounce) your left hip forward two bounces, then your right hip backward two bounces, then your left hip forward one bounce, and your right hip backward one bounce.

6. Shift your weight back onto your left leg, then hitch your right knee up and swivel your left foot a quarter turn to the left.

7. Begin the steps again with your right foot and repeat the steps until the end of the song.

> **Teacher Tip:** You may wish to search the Internet for videos of these and other dances.

Dance Music Suggestions

"La cucaracha" by The Gipsy Kings (Mexican)

"Mucho Mambo Sway" by Shaft (Latino)

"Jump in the Line" by Harry Belafonte (Calypso)

"Rock Lobster" by the B-52s (70s)

"Footloose" by Kenny Loggins (80s)

"Pony Time" by Chubby Checker (60s)

"Clarinet Polka" by Walter Ostanek

"Paddy Fahy's Jig" by Kevin Burke (Irish)

"In the Mood" by The Glen Miller Orchestra (swing)

"Let's Get Loud" by Jennifer Lopez (Salsa)

"Décalé Gwada" by Jessy Matador (African)

"The Wah-Watusi" by The Orlons (60s)

"At the Hop" by Danny and the Juniors (50s)

"Pennsylvania Polka" by Frankie Yankovic

"Diggy Liggy Lo" by John Fogarty (East Coast)

"I Like to Move It, Move It" by Sacha Baron Cohen

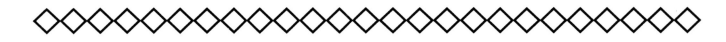

QDPA Ideas—Hooping

Activity Level: moderate to vigorous

Hooping is a challenging low-impact aerobic activity that improves coordination, flexibility, and endurance, as well as strengthens the core muscles. Hooping is a flexible physical activity that can be done individually or in small or large groups. Hooping is also fun and easy to learn!

Hooping

What you need:

• a plastic hoop for each participant

What you do:

1. Demonstrate for students how to place the hoop over their head and position the hoop around their waist.

2. Remind students to grip the hoop with both hands. Model for students how to extend your arms out from your body, and slightly forward.

3. Next have students stand with their feet shoulder-width apart and have them press the hoop against their lower back.

4. With the hoop still pressing against your back, demonstrate how to move the hoop and your arms side to side. Move your hips around in a circle. While doing this, keep the hoop pressed against your back.

5. When ready, demonstrate how to fling the hoop hard to the left or right with both hands, then let it go so it starts to go around your body.

6. Demonstrate for students how to move your hips in a circle quickly to keep the hoop rotating around your body.

7. Reinforce with students that the more you move your hips, the faster the hoop will go around your body.

8. If students are having difficulty keeping the hoop rotating, encourage them to keep practicing and validate their efforts.

Hooping Contest

Give each player a hoop. Have them practice rotating it around their waist. Have a contest to see who can hoop for the longest time without dropping it.

QDPA—Hoop Games
Activity Level: moderate to vigorous

Hoop Toss

1. Set up pylons at various positions around the activity area.
2. Put players into small groups and have them line up and toss the hoop to try to ring a pylon.
3. As players become more skilled at ringing the pylons, move players farther away from the pylons.
4. Put a sticky note or tape a sign on each pylon to assign it a point value, with the highest point value on the pylons that are farthest away.
5. Each player can have three tries to ring a pylon with the hoop.
6. Record their points. The player with the highest points wins.

Hoop It Everywhere!

1. When players know how to rotate a hoop around their waist, encourage them to try rotating the hoop around other parts of their body, such as their neck, wrist, arm, knees, and ankle.
2. Encourage players to keep practicing until they can do it!

Through the Hoop

1. Divide players into equal teams. Give the first player in each team a hoop.
2. Tell players they must start by holding the hoop above their head. They must then pass the hoop down over their body from their head to their toes, then step out of the hoop and pass it to the next team member who then passes the hoop over their own body.
3. When the hoop gets to the last team member and that member has stepped out of the hoop, they will then switch directions. The last team member must then step *into* the hoop and pass it *up* their body from their feet to their head, then give it to the next team member. They must move the hoop up through the team in this manner and back to the first player.
4. The first team to pass the hoop all the way back to the first player wins.

Variation: Have players pass the hoop over their body while sitting on the ground. They must not stand up or get on their feet at any time, but they can lift their bottom off the ground and shift their body to move the hoop past.

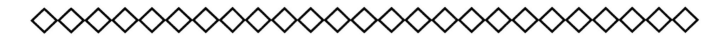

QDPA—Crab Walking Games
Activity Level: moderate to vigorous

Crab walking is a very unusual, challenging, and fun way to move. The muscles of the body are basically working in the opposite way to what they usually do. Crab walking increases the breathing rate and heart rate, improves coordination and concentration, and stretches and builds the muscles of the arms, shoulders, back, buttocks, ankles, and legs.

Racing Crabs

1. Establish a starting line, with a finish line about 10 metres away.

2. Divide players into 2 or 3 equal groups of no more than 10 each. Choose one group to go first.

3. Have the group of players line up side by side at the starting line. On "Ready. Set. Go!" they must crab walk as quickly as they can to the finish line.

4. The winner from that group will later compete with the winners from the other two groups until there is just one winner.

Beanbag Crab Race

1. Establish a starting line, with a finish line about 10 metres away.

2. Divide players into 5 or 6 equal groups and have players line up in their groups at the starting line. There should be about 2 metres of space between groups.

3. Give each group 6 beanbags, and have them place the beanbags in a pile near the starting line for use as the game progresses.

4. Tell players they will crab walk from the starting line to the finish line, carrying a beanbag on their belly, then stand up and run back to their group, put the beanbag back in the pile, and go to the end of the line.

5. The next player can start as soon as the previous player has reached the finish line. When all the players have had a turn with 1 beanbag, they then make the trip with 2 beanbags, then with 3 beanbags. The first team to have all members finish the race with 3 beanbags wins.

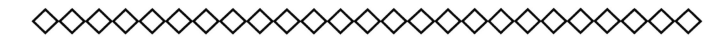

QDPA—Single Jump-Rope Skills
Activity Level: vigorous

Jumping rope is an excellent way for students to get cardiovascular exercise and to practice their coordination skills. Once experienced, students will enjoy experimenting with different jump-rope moves or jumping rope to music.

Use the following steps to help students learn to jump rope:

1. First, model for students how to hop with both feet side by side, and shoulder-width apart. Once students have mastered the skill, model how to hop-bounce. Learning to hop-bounce with help students time the turning of the jump rope.

2. Next demonstrate for students how to swing the rope. Show students how to hold the jump rope handles firmly, one in each hand with thumbs pointing down. Then swing the rope over your head so it lands in front of you, then step over the rope. Highlight for students how to make small circles with your wrists while turning the rope.

3. Encourage students to make just one jump at a time. Eventually students can add the hop-bounce when comfortable. Remind students to not jump while the rope is in the air. Instead the rope should hit the floor in front of the student before they try to jump the rope. In addition, during jumping, stress to students that the rope should touch the floor surface gently.

4. Expect that some students will need lots of practice simply stepping over the rope while they turn the rope. Jumping the rope will come in time.

5. Note that the proper form for jumping rope is to stay on the balls of the feet and the toes while jumping, not on flat feet.

6. Emphasize for students the importance of keeping their head erect and looking straight ahead while jumping rope to keep balanced.

QDPA—Single Jump-Rope Activities
Activity Level: vigorous

Tip: Jump Rope For Heart

To learn more jump-rope techniques, visit the Jump Rope For Heart website and access animated demonstrations of various skipping techniques. This website is sponsored by the Heart and Stroke Foundation. Your school may also wish to run a Jump Rope For Heart event.
http://www.jumpropeforheart.ca/kids-getskipping.asp#

Follow the Leader

Follow the leader! Challenge students to follow your lead and try different jump-rope moves. Do 5 of each move to start. When students get used to the jump-rope moves, increase to 10 of each. The use of music can be an effective motivator for students to set the tempo for their jumping.

Here are some suggested jump-rope moves. Use your imagination and add more moves!

Basic Jump: hop-bounce in place with both feet together

Hip Twist: twist your lower body from side to side, jumping once on each side

Double-Leg Jump: jump over the rotating rope with both feet at the same time

Front Straddles: put one foot forward and the other foot back, like a scissor jump, then switch feet while jumping up

Hop: hop on one foot for 5 jumps, then hop on the other foot

High Knees: bring knees up high one at a time with each jump

Cross Jumps: cross one foot in front of the other, then switch and cross the other foot in front, switch for each jump

Big Jumps: jump high with each jump

Rope Sweeps: continue jumping while you bring both hands together in front of you; sweep the rope to the left side of your body, right side, left, right, then open the rope and jump back in on the 5th beat

Turn Around: with each jump, do a quarter turn

Chalkboard Publishing © 2013

QDPA—Single Jump-Rope Activities (cont'd)
Activity Level: vigorous

Kick It: kick one foot forward for one jump while hopping on the other foot, then switch feet

Tiny Jumps: make your jumps very small so your feet are not raised very far off the ground

Tall Jumps: stretch your body up tall and hold the position while jumping

Short Jumps: squat as low as you can and hold the position while jumping; challenge players to see how low they can jump while still turning the rope

Forward and Back: while jumping with both feet together, move forward two jumps, jump once in place, then move back two jumps

Running in Place: run in place while jumping the rope

Running Forward and Back: jump rope while running slowly forward for the count of 5, run in place for the count of 5, then run slowly backward for the count of 5

Alternating Feet: start with your left foot on the ground and your right foot lifted slightly off the ground, then jump the rope with your right foot while lifting your left foot to let the rope pass; shift your weight back onto your left foot before the rope comes back around

More challenging moves to use at your discretion

Alternating Jumps: while jumping on your toes, alternate putting one foot forward for each jump like boxers do, but do not let that foot touch the ground; if players find this difficult, they can tap the toes of their front foot on the ground each time

Cross Uncross: cross your arms for one jump so the rope crosses, then uncross for the next jump, then cross, then uncross

Crossed Arms: keep arms crossed while turning the rope for 5 jumps

Backward Turning: turn the rope backward while jumping in place

Side Straddles: move your legs out to the sides for one jump, and back together for the next jump, as in jumping jacks; make sure you keep your toes pointed forward

Double Under: for every jump, the rope must do two revolutions, so jump high

---

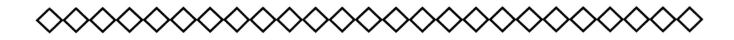

QDPA—Chair Aerobics

Activity Level: moderate to vigorous

Chair aerobics improve balance, flexibility, circulation, and muscle strength. These low-impact activities are perfect for the classroom on rainy days or when another facility is not available. Before starting:

- Remind students to be careful to stay in their personal space while they are moving.
- If possible, have students move their chairs a few feet away from their desk so they can stretch their legs out while sitting on the edge of their chair.
- Ensure that students keep their backs straight while doing the activities.
- Consider playing music during the activities.
- Make sure that the chairs are stable and will not tip or slide when weight is applied to the front edge.

Teacher Call-Out Instructions

Front Kick: Hold your chair seat with both hands. Lift your right leg out straight in front and down again. Now lift your right leg out straight in front and down again. Switch legs!

Biking: Hold the chair seat with both hands, and pedal your feet and legs as though you are riding a bike. Pedal faster. Faster! Now pedal backward.

Paddling: Pretend you are paddling a canoe for 5 strokes on your left side, then on your right side.

Swimming: Bend forward and move your arms as though you are swimming on your front. Then change to swimming on your back. Lean back and do the flutter kick with your feet. Then jump up from your chair and sit back down, as though you were bobbing in the water.

Hiking: Swing your arms at your sides and lift your knees high as though you are hiking, and reach left and right while tapping your toes on the floor. Then stand and face your chair. March in place, raising your knees high, tapping your toes on the chair, and swinging your arms at your sides.

Scissors: Hold the chair seat with both hands. Raise both legs in front of you and do 5 scissors at waist height. Lower your feet and raise your arms and do 5 overhead scissors with your arms. Lower your arms and reach them over the back of the chair, stretching as far as you can. Then bend over and reach your arms under the front of the chair, stretching as far as you can.

Twist: Keeping a straight back and your hands on your hips, twist your upper body to the right and hold for 5 seconds. Then twist your upper body to the left.

Variation—Simon Says: Choose a player to take on the role of "Simon," calling out instructions for players to follow. Instructions should only be followed only if the instruction is prefaced with the expression, "Simon says."

QDPA—Fitness Circuit Activities

Activity Level: vigorous

Students will enjoy the challenge of circuit training where a number of fitness stations are arranged in a circuit in a space such as a hallway, classroom, gymnasium, or outdoors. Students must complete a set of physical activities before moving on to the next fitness station.

Teacher Tips

- Review and display for students posters explaining the expectations of each station.
- Emphasize for students the importance of correct technique when participating.
- Establish signals for starting, stopping, and rotating through the fitness circuit, for example, a whistle, hand clap, verbal signals, etc.
- Keep students' heart rates up by timing each fitness station so that each student is active for 30–60 seconds.
- Ideally students should have no more than a one minute break between each fitness station.
- Have students record their heart rate at the beginning and end of the class.
- You may wish to have students set personal goals for themselves and then reflect on how they did.

Sample Fitness Circuit Stations

Standing Long Jump: Stand with your feet together. Jump as far forward from the starting line as you can and repeat in the time allowed.

Line Jumping: Jump back and forth across a line or rope as many times as you can in the time allowed.

Slalom Dribbling: Follow the circuit, and dribble around the pylons using a basketball or soccer ball. Return to the start and repeat as many times as you can during the time allowed.

Slalom Stick Handling: Follow the circuit, and stick handle around the pylons using a hockey stick and ball. Return to the start and repeat as many times as you can during the time allowed.

One-Foot Hops: Hop 15 times on one foot, then hop 15 times on the other foot and repeat for as long as you can during time allowed.

Jumping Jacks: Complete as many jumping jacks as you can during time allowed.

Owl Hop: Stand on one leg and hook your other foot behind the knee of the standing leg. Keep your foot in place while you squat down and jump forward as far as you can. Change legs and try again.

High Knees: Bend your arms at the elbows and hold your hands forward at waist height, palms down. Run in place, bringing your knees up to touch the palms of your hands with each step as many times as you can during the time allowed.

Squats: Stand with your feet shoulder-width apart and arms straight out in front. Bend your knees until you are in a sitting position. Hold for 5 seconds. Stand up again and repeat as many times as you can during the time allowed.

Skipping on the spot: Jump rope with both feet together to start, then alternate onto each foot. You may also try different moves. Jump rope for as long as you can during the time allowed.

Leg Claps: Lift one knee high and clap your hands together under your leg. Repeat with your other leg. Keep alternating legs for as long as you can during the time allowed.

Burpees: Start in squat position and crouch down until your hands are touching the ground directly in front of you. Then kick your feet back into a plank position and complete a push-up. Next quickly jump your feet back into a squat position and jump straight up in the air. Clap your hands over your head. Repeat as many times as you can during the time allowed.

Running Laps: Run around the course and count the total number of laps you can complete in the time allowed.

> **Teacher Tip:** You may also wish to place students into small groups and have them create their own fitness circuit for the class to try.

How to Check Your Heart Rate

Daily physical activity makes your heart beat faster, which exercises and strengthens your heart. The heart is a muscle that pumps blood out around the body. Pulse points are places on your body where you can feel your heart pumping. A heart rate is the number of heartbeats or beats per minute (BPM). Your pulse beats match your heartbeat so you can find out your heart rate. Before, during, and after daily physical activity, check your heart rate by counting your pulse. Here are two ways you can find your pulse.

On Your Neck

1. Put three fingers of your left hand on the right side of your neck about halfway between your Adam's apple and the side of your neck. (Your Adam's apple is the bump at the front of your neck that moves up and down when you swallow.)

2. Keep moving your fingers a little at a time until you feel a pulse beat. It may help to move your fingers up closer to your jaw.

On Your Wrist

1. Stick your thumb up in the air and turn the palm of your hand facing you.

2. Next, slide the first two fingers of your other hand down the side of your thumb until your fingers reach your wrist.

3. Let your fingers slide downward onto the inside of your wrist, and gently feel for your pulse. You should feel a beat where your fingers touch the front of your wrist, just below your thumb.

4. If you have trouble finding your pulse, try bending your wrist back a little.

How to Calculate Your Heart Rate

1. When you have found a steady beat, count how many beats there are in 15 seconds (use a watch or clock with a second hand).

2. Then multiply that number by 4 to find out how many beats there would be in 1 minute.

Normal heart rate for children age 6–15: 70–100 beats per minute

Target heart rate when exercising: 220 – your age = predicted maximum heart rate

---

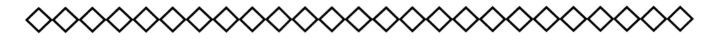

Daily Physical Activity Journal

Name _____

Remember to calculate your heart rate by counting the beats in 15 seconds, then multiplying by 4 to get the beats per minute. Check your target heart rate to see how you are doing!

How am I doing?

Activity	Your Heart Rate (BPM)		
	Before the Activity	During the Activity	After the Activity

Yoga
Activity Level: moderate

Yoga is a wonderful form of exercise to calm the mind, and warm, stretch, and strengthen the muscles and body. Slow movements gently increase breathing and blood flow, which in turn fuels the muscles and tissues and increases flexibility. Students benefit from gentle stretching and movement that is done in a calm and quiet manner, leaving students feeling calm, peaceful, flexible, and ready to take on more vigorous and strenuous activities. Remember that every body is different, so each student's pose might also look a little different from their neighbour's pose. The emphasis should not be on performing perfect poses, and should be adapted as needed for individual students.

Getting Started

- Ideally, students should wear comfortable clothing and practice in bare feet on individual yoga mats or on a smooth non-slippery surface.

- You may want to set the tone for yoga by playing soft, soothing music.

- Ensure that students have enough personal space to participate.

- Be a good role model and always demonstrate the postures for students, rather than just explaining what to do.

- Do not expect students to remember how to do the various postures. Be patient and review. You may ask students to show and explain the poses they know.

About Breathing

- Breathing deeply and steadily is important in yoga because it gives us energy for our body, and keeps us calm and focused.

- Remember to breathe in through your nose, down into your belly. Feel your belly get bigger as you breathe in, and get smaller again as you breathe out.

- Try to always breathe out through your nose. If you are working really hard, you may need to breath out through your mouth.

More Ideas

- Encourage students to be creative and invent their own unique poses and movements. Invite students to teach their peers their creations.

- Tell imaginative stories as a springboard for doing different yoga poses. For example, pretend you are going on a trip through the forest. Do poses such as a Eagle, Frog, etc., as they come up in the story.

Eagle Pose

In Eagle Pose, we will twist our arms and legs around each other, stretch our upper back, and challenge our balance.

1. Stand tall with your arms at your sides.
2. Place your right arm over your left arm and bend your elbows upward.
3. Twist your arms around each other; try to make your palms touch. If they don't reach all the way, that is okay. (Option: The back of your left hand against the outer side of your right elbow.)
4. Bend your knees and lift your left foot off the floor.
5. Twist your left leg around your right leg.
6. Hook your left foot around the lower part of your right leg if you can. (Option: The toes of your left foot can be on the floor for balance.)
7. Lift your left hip up slightly to square your pelvis, then squeeze your inner thighs together for balance. Pull your belly button to your spine and tuck your tailbone under to help you stay strong and steady.
8. Breathe deeply and try to sit down lower into your legs, keeping your weight in your heel. Try to lift your arms higher to stretch your upper back.
9. Keep looking straight ahead.
10. Breathe in to return to standing. Breathe out to unravel your body.
11. Repeat the pose with your left arm and your right leg.

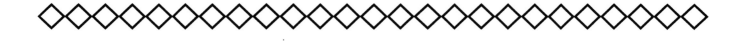

Downward-Facing Dog Pose

We are going to get down on the floor, lift our hips up high, and let our head hang underneath our bodies, like a dog stretching.

1. Go down on your hands and knees like a dog.
2. Breathe out, curl your toes under, and straighten your legs. Lift your dog tail into the air.
3. Breathe in, lift your bottom higher.
4. Breathe out and press your heels and hands into the floor.
5. Pretend you are a dog stretching its front legs and wagging its tail.

Three-Legged Dog Pose

We are going to get down on the floor, lift our hips up high, then lift one leg up off the floor like a dog stretching its leg.

1. Go down on your hands and knees.
2. Breathe out, and curl your toes under as you straighten your knees. Lift your hips so your bottom is up.
3. Breathe in and lift your left leg straight out behind you. Hold it up.
4. Breathe out and lower your left leg so your foot is back on the floor.
5. Repeat with your right leg.

Mountain Pose

Let's stand tall like a mighty mountain.

1. Stand tall with feet together, or feet wider apart. Point your toes forward.
2. Have your arms down at your sides.
3. Press your shoulders back.
4. Make your body tall, straight, and strong, like a mighty mountain.
5. Breathe in and out deeply and slowly.

Crocodile Pose

Let's lift our chest like a crocodile opening its mouth.

1. Lie on your belly with your forehead touching the ground, your feet stretched out behind you, and squeezing your bottom.
2. Bring your arms in front of your head, then place each hand on your arm at the elbow. Rest your forehead on your arms.
3. Breathe in through your nose as you lift your chest from the ground nice and high like when a crocodile is opening its big mouth.
4. Breathe out as you bring your upper body back to the floor.

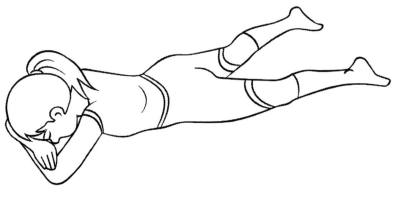

Ragdoll Pose

Let's fold our chest down over our legs and let our upper body hang loose like a floppy ragdoll.

1. Stand up straight and tall.
2. Breathe in and reach your arms up to the sky. Lift your kneecaps up with the front of your thighs to make your legs strong.
3. Breathe out and fold your upper body forward. Tip your hips and pelvis forward to keep your lower back straight. Lift your belly button up toward your spine as you fold to protect your back.
4. Let your arms and head hang loose toward the floor like a floppy ragdoll. Nod your head "yes," then shake your head "no" to relax your neck.
5. Ideally, your legs should be straight, with the front of your thighs strong and your pelvis tilting forward. If you cannot do this, bend your knees a little to be more comfortable.
6. Take deep breaths into your lower back. As you breathe out, let your arms and body drop closer to the floor.
7. To come back up to standing, bend your knees, breathe in, and slowly roll your body back up until you are standing straight.

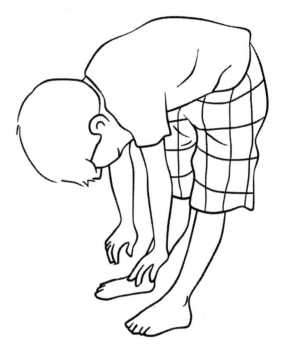

Camel Pose

Let's lift up our chest high like the hump of a camel.

1. Go on your knees on the floor with your feet flat out behind you, toenails on the floor.
2. Keep your body straight.
3. Place the palm of your hands on your lower back. Squeeze your bottom as you push your hips forward. Try to keep your hips over your knees.
4. Gently look up and arch your back and reach back behind you until your hands are touching your heels or the bottoms of your feet.
5. Lift your chest like a camel's hump.

Shooting Stars Breathing Exercise

Let's make stars twinkle as they shoot through the sky.

1. Sit strong and tall, and pull your belly button to your spine. Cross your legs.
2. As you breathe in, reach your hands up above your head, palms facing each other.
3. As you breathe out, wiggle your fingers like little stars twinkling, while you slowly bring your hands back down with your arms out wide.
4. Repeat.

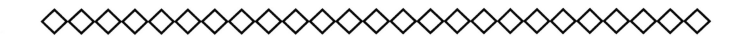

Frog Pose

Let's squat like a frog ready to leap over a log.

1. Stand with your feet shoulder-width apart, and squat down.
2. While balancing on your toes, keep your knees spread wide apart.
3. Put your hands on the floor between your knees.
4. Look straight ahead and breathe in.
5. As you breathe out, keep you hands on the floor while you straighten your legs so your bottom goes up. Lower your head toward your knees.
6. Come back to the squatting position, and repeat.

Lion Pose

Let's become a lion, the mighty king of the jungle.

1. Kneel on the floor and sit back on your feet.
2. Place your hands on your thighs and stretch your arms.
3. Spread your fingers, flare your nostrils, and open your eyes wide.
4. Open your mouth wide like a big lion yawning and stick out your tongue.
5. Curl the tip of your tongue toward your chin. Breathe in deeply.
6. Exhale with a roar just like a mighty lion!

Fish Pose

Let's puff out our chest like a fish breathing through its gills.

1. Lie on the floor on your back, with your knees bent and your feet flat on the floor.
2. Lift your bottom slightly off the floor. Slide your hands, palms down, under your bottom and move your arms under your body. Lower your body so your bottom sits on the backs of your hands.
3. Press your forearms and elbows firmly against the floor. Squeeze your shoulder blades together.
4. Take a breath in. Arch your back to lift your back and head away from the floor.
5. Gently let the crown or back of your head rest on the floor. Keep your head touching the floor only very lightly to avoid hurting your neck. Press your heels forward. Keep the weight on your elbows to keep the weight off your head.
6. Imagine you are breathing through fish gills.
7. Breathe out. Press into your elbows again and slide your head gently back, returning your body and head to the floor.

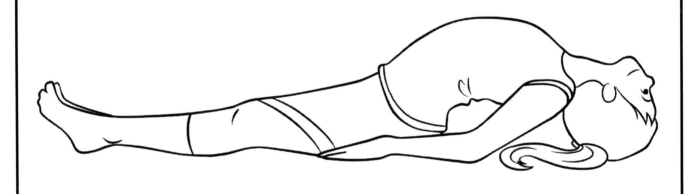

Bow Pose

Let's turn our body into a bow that is getting ready to shoot an arrow.

1. Lie on your belly with your arms beside your body and your palms facing up.
2. Breathe out and bend your knees, bringing your feet as close to your bottom as possible. Squeeze your bottom to lengthen your lower back.

3. Reach back with your hands and grab hold of your ankles. Keep your knees hip-width apart.
4. Breathe in. Lift your heels toward the sky, and lift your thighs, chin, and chest.
5. Look forward as you arch your back like a bow. Now you just need an arrow!

Dolphin Pose

Let's make our body look like a dolphin who is swimming and jumping in the waves.

1. Go on your hands and knees on the floor, with your arms shoulder-width apart like a tabletop.

2. Lower your upper body so your forearms and the palms of your hands are flat on the floor in front of you. Your hands, arms, and elbows should all be shoulder-width apart.

3. Breathe out as you curl your toes under and lift your knees off the floor.

4. Try to press your heels to the floor.

5. Bring your bottom up high toward the sky so your body makes an upside down V shape like a swimming dolphin jumping over waves.

6. Keep your head between your arms and try to look at your knees.

7. Hold the pose and breathe calmly.

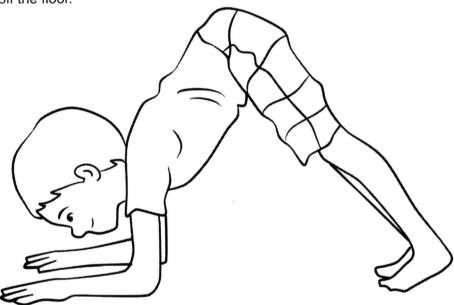

Chair Pose

We can make our legs strong by pretending to sit back into a chair.

1. Stand with your feet together, your big toes touching. Lift your toes to keep your weight safely in your heels.

2. Breathe in and reach your arms up over your head.

3. Breathe out, bend your knees, and bring your upper body forward. Bring your bottom down and push your hips back as though you were going to sit in a chair.

4. Reach up with your arms all the way into your fingertips. Your arms will now be pointing forward at an angle.

5. Keep your back straight by pulling your belly button in.

6. Try to bring your thighs down a little so they are parallel to the floor. Hold the pose and breathe deeply.

7. Breathe in and straighten your legs until you are standing up straight again.

8. Breathe out and lower your arms down to your sides.

Flower Pose

Let's sit on the ground and lift our legs and heart up like the petals of a flower.

1. Sit tall on the floor with your knees wide apart and the bottoms of your feet together.
2. Bring both hands forward between your knees, and turn your palms up.
3. Slide your hands under your ankles, keeping your palms facing up.
4. Use your hands to lift your ankles and feet up off the floor. Keep your knees wide apart.
5. Lean your body back a bit until you are balancing on your tailbone.
6. Lift your ankles up so your feet are off the floor and your body is balanced on your tailbone.
7. Breathe in and lift your chest up. Feel like a flower blooming toward the sun.

Table Pose

Let's make a table that is strong and stable.

1. Go on your hands and knees on the floor.
2. Put your knees and feet hip-width apart and right below your hips.
3. Put your hands below your shoulders, shoulder-width apart.
4. Face your palms down and spread your fingers wide.
5. Look at the floor directly below you. Breathe calmly and hold.
6. Lift your belly button up to your spine so your table is flat and strong.
7. Could you balance a tray of glasses on your table?

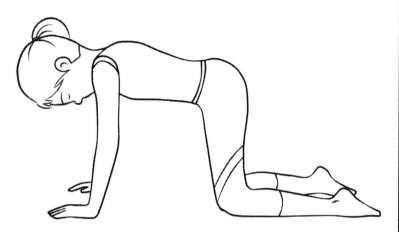

Butterfly Pose

Let's spread your butterfly wings.

1. Sit on the floor with your knees bent and the bottoms of your feet together.
2. Hold your feet together with your hands. Your elbows can be between your legs or resting on your knees.
3. Keep your back nice and straight. Pull your belly button in to your spine.
4. Breathe deeply as you gently press your knees down like a butterfly opening its wings.

Plank Pose

Let's make our bodies strong and straight, like a board plank.

1. Get on the floor on your hands and knees, on the floor, with your arms shoulder-width apart like a tabletop.
2. Breathe out, and bring your feet back as you straighten your knees.
3. Pull your belly button to your spine to keep your back and belly strong.

4. Lower your bottom until it is in a straight line with your legs and back.
5. Keep your belly button pulled to your spine to keep your plank flat as a board.

Option: You can bring your knees down instead of putting your legs out straight, especially if this pose hurts your wrists.

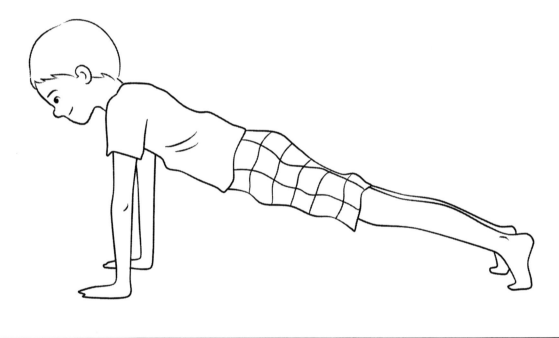

Triangle Pose

Let's make a big strong triangle with our bodies.

1. Stand up tall with your feet spread comfortably wide apart (about a leg's length).

2. Turn your right foot out so it points straight to the side, and turn your left foot in just a little. Make the heel of your right foot line up with the arch of your left foot.

3. Make your legs strong; feel like you are lifting your kneecaps up with the front of your thigh. Lift the arches of your feet and your ankles.

4. Breathe in deeply as you lift your arms to shoulder height, palms facing the floor. Tuck your bottom under and be strong in your belly muscles.

5. As you breathe out, bend your body to the right from the hips, keeping your spine long and straight without tilting forward or backward.

6. Place your right hand on your thigh, calf, or ankle (not on your knee). Choose a spot that feels comfortable and allows you to keep your body flat and straight.

7. Reach your left arm toward the sky. Keep reaching up through your fingertips.

8. You can face forward, or try looking up to your top hand or down to your bottom hand.

9. Make long beautiful lines in your triangle; arms are straight from bottom to top, legs straight and strong, spine straight and waist long.

10. Hold the pose and breathe. In the triangle pose, we are building strength and flexibility at the same time.

11. To come back up, bend your right leg (front leg), breath in deeply and lift your upper body back to standing, arms up over your head.

12. Breathe out as you bring your arms back down to your sides and straighten your feet forward.

13. Repeat to the left side.

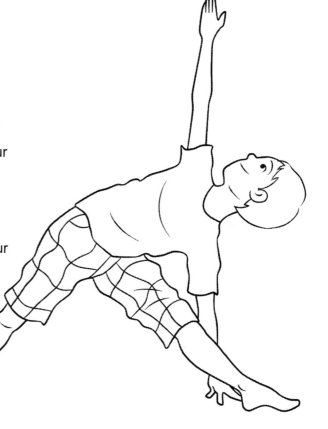

Rainbow Pose

Let's show off all the beautiful colours of the rainbow.

1. Either kneeling or standing, breathe in while raising both arms over your head.

2. Lower one arm. Slowly breathe out as you sweep the other arm over your head toward the opposite shoulder to make a rainbow shape.

3. Hold this position. Pull in your belly button to keep your rainbow big, beautiful, and bright. Show off all the colours!

4. Breathe in as you slowly straighten your body and return to the starting position.

5. Now make a rainbow with your other arm.

Quality Daily Physical Activity

Teamwork Award

_____

Quality Daily Physical Activity

Great Effort Award

_____

QDPA Planner—Week of _____

Monday	Warm-up:
When: _____	Activity:
Where: _____	Cool-down:
	Notes:

Tuesday	Warm-up:
When: _____	Activity:
Where: _____	Cool-down:
	Notes:

Wednesday	Warm-up:
When: _____	Activity:
Where: _____	Cool-down:
	Notes:

Thursday	Warm-up:
When: _____	Activity:
Where: _____	Cool-down:
	Notes:

Friday	Warm-up:
When: _____	Activity:
Where: _____	Cool-down:
	Notes:

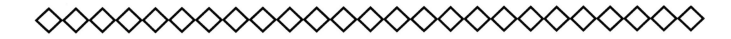

QDPA Class List

Student's Name	Participation	Fair Play and Sportsmanship	Safety	Overall Mark

QDPA Self-Check: How am I doing?

Name _____

Physical Signs of Moderate Effort	Yes	No	Not Sure
I feel my heart beating a little faster.			
I am breathing a little faster.			
I can still talk to someone comfortably.			
My body feels warmer.			

Physical Signs of Vigorous Effort	Yes	No	Not Sure
I feel my heart beating a lot faster.			
I am breathing a lot faster.			
I am finding it hard to talk to someone comfortably.			
I am starting to feel out of breath.			
My body feels very warm.			
I am starting to sweat.			

QDPA Success Criteria Rubric

Student _____

	Level 1	Level 2	Level 3	Level 4
Participation	Student rarely displays effort and participation during QDPA.	Student occasionally displays effort and participation during QDPA.	Student usually displays effort and participation during QDPA.	Student consistently displays effort and participation during QDPA.
Fair Play and Sportsmanship	Student needs encouragement to be a team player.	Student occasionally shares, helps, and encourages others.	Student usually shares, helps, and encourages others.	Student consistently shares, helps, and encourages others.
Safety	Student requires constant reminders regarding safety or the safe use of equipment and facilities.	Student requires some reminders regarding safety or the safe use of equipment and facilities.	Student requires few reminders regarding safety or the safe use of equipment and facilities.	Student requires almost no reminders regarding safety or the safe use of equipment and facilities.

Teacher Comments:

_____

_____

_____

_____